Questions that Work

A Resource for Facilitators

by

Dorothy Strachan

ST Press
Ottawa
Canada

National Library of Canada Cataloguing in Publication Data

Strachan, Dorothy, 1947-
        Questions that work: a resource for facilitators

(ST Press Facilitation Series)
Includes bibliographical references.
ISBN #0-9688036-0-1

        1. Organizational learning. I. Title. II. Series.

HD58.82.S83 2001   658.3'124   C2001-900703-5

Production: Peter Ashley

Copy Editor: Heather Ebbs, Editor's Ink

Design: David Farrar, Farrar Graphics, Ottawa, Ontario

Printing: Lowe-Martin Group, Ottawa, Ontario

ST Press books are available at special discounts to use as premiums and sales promotions or for use in corporate training programs.

For information about other ST Press resources, please contact us or go to our web site at www.stpress.ca.

ST Press
31 Euclid Avenue
Ottawa, Canada
K1S 2W2
Phone: 613-730-1000
Fax: 613-730-0014
email: stpress@cyberus.ca

Contents

Acknowledgements i

Preface iii
   Are You a Facilitator? iii
   Finding the Right Questions iv

How to Use This Handbook v
   About Words vi
   Tell Us What You Think vii

Part I: How to Ask Questions 1

Chapter 1 – Making Questions Work 3
   Constructing Questions 4
   Types of Questions 5
      Closed questions 5
      Open questions 7
   Guiding Principles 8
      1. Customize for context 8
      2. Create inviting questions 10
      3. Ask with sensitivity 12
      4. Accommodate risk 13
      5. Prepare participants for tough questions 15
      6. Ask follow-up questions 16
   Dos and Don'ts 19
   Recommended Reading 23

Chapter 2 – Core Facilitation Values 25
   Integrity 26
      Confirm roles of chair and facilitator 26
      Clarify confidentiality 27
      Be sensitive to conflict of interest 28
      Avoid collusion 28
      Ask questions ethically 29
      Avoid intrusive questions 30
      Address imbalances in power and information 30

Chapter 2 (continued)

Mutual Respect 32
    Respect exchange times 33
    Be patient – whose silence is it? 33
    Encourage direct interaction 34
    Don't ask for facts 34
    Model mutual respect 34

Authenticity 35
    Build group ownership for outcomes 36
    Minimize self-deception 36
    Be clear about intentions 37
    Acknowledge problems 38

Closing Thoughts: Leaning on Values 38

Recommended Reading 39

Part II: What To Ask When 41

    Introduction 43

Chapter 3 – Questions for Opening a Session 45

    Guidelines for Opening Questions 46

    Getting to Know One Another 49
        Focus: Sharing personal information 49
        Focus: Work experience 52

    Setting Group Norms 54
        Focus: Ground rules 54
        Focus: Building ownership 57

    Clarifying Expectations 59
        Focus: Hopes and concerns 59
        Focus: Objectives and outcomes 61

    Recommended Reading 63

Chapter 4 – Questions for Enabling Action 65

    Guidelines for Using the "What? – So What? – Now What?" Framework . . . 68

    "What?" – The Notice Questions: Observations 70

    "So What?" – The Meaning Questions: Reflections 73
        Focus: Meaning and fit 73
        Focus: Organizations and the nature of work 76
        Focus: Personal development 79

Chapter 4 (continued)

"Now What?" – The Application Questions: Action 81
    Focus: Personal change 81
    Focus: Organizational change 84
    Focus: Building ownership 85
    Focus: Operational planning and implementation 87

Recommended Reading 89

Chapter 5 – Questions for Thinking Critically 91

Guidelines for Questions on Thinking Critically 94

Making Assumptions and Perspectives Explicit 96
    Focus: The individual 96
    Focus: The organization 98
    Focus: The broader context 101

Understanding Interests and Power Relationships 104
    Focus: The individual 104
    Focus: The organization 106
    Focus: The broader context 108

Exploring Alternative Ways of Thinking and Acting 110
    Focus: The individual 110
    Focus: The organization 113
    Focus: The broader context 115

Doing the Right Thing 117
    Focus: The individual 118
    Focus: The organization 120
    Focus: The broader context 123

Recommended Reading 124

Chapter 6 – Questions for Addressing Issues 125

Guidelines for Addressing Issues 127

Identifying the Issues 129

Understanding the Issues 132

Generating Options for Action 136

Testing Options for Action 138

Making a Decision 140

Taking Action 143

Recommended Reading 145

Chapter 7 — Questions For Closing a Session 147
  Guidelines for Closing Questions 148
  Reflecting on the Process 150
    Focus: Perspectives on the experience 150
    Focus: Midway through a Process 154
    Focus: Productivity 155
    Focus: Celebrating success 157
  Considering Next Steps 159
  Debriefing 161
  Recommended Reading 163

Chapter 8 — Questions for Specific Cases 165
  Opening a Workshop on a Specific Topic 165
  Opening a Series of Workshops 169
  Bringing a Project to a Close 171
  Closing a National, Issues-based Workshop 173
  Conducting Exit Interviews in Small Groups 175
  Enabling a Structured Approach to Reflection and Action 178
  Encouraging Candour and Confidentiality 180
  Exploring Legislation That Impacts on Organizational Policies 182
  Loosening Up A Tight Group 184
  Putting Sensitive Issues on the Table 186
  Reflecting on and Applying Research 187
  Reviewing a Pilot Workshop 190
  Supporting Action After a Meeting of a Network or Coalition 192
  Thinking Critically About Policy Changes 194
  Workplace Stress: Encouraging Candour and Action 198

Endnotes 201

Acknowledgements

Sincere thanks to the following colleagues and friends who reviewed earlier versions of this manuscript and provided helpful feedback:

Fil Alfonso, Asian Institute of Management

Susan Berlin, Facilitator in Private Practice

Randy Brooks, Facilitator in Private Practice

Brenda Chartrand, Conference Board of Canada

Peggy Edwards, Writer and Facilitator, The Alder Group

Jo Hauser, Physician, Consultant and Manager

Eric Pitters, Sales Executive and Coach

Marian Pitters, Facilitator in Private Practice

Sue Potter, Facilitator in Private Practice

Hilda Sabadash, Bereaved Families of Ontario, Ottawa region

Elinor Wilson, Heart and Stroke Foundation of Canada

Marc Wilson, Canadian Broadcasting Corporation.

This book is just one of many things that my partner, Paul Tomlinson, makes possible.

For the Rider and the Rower

Preface

Being a facilitator has consumed a good part of my life. I started out as a high school teacher and then moved into the community college system as a teacher and administrator before venturing into professional facilitation as the principal in a small consulting firm.

Today I am a partner in Strachan•Tomlinson, an Ottawa-based management consulting company. A large part of what we have been doing for the past 25 years focuses on the design and facilitation of group processes in areas such as strategic planning, team development, policy development, organizational change, and training for facilitators and trainers. We work with a variety of clients in the public, private and not-for-profit sectors at local, regional, national and international levels.

My business partner is Paul Tomlinson. Paul's primary expertise is in program review and in gathering and developing the background information that informs our facilitation efforts. He does this through research processes and diagnostics such as interviews, surveys, questionnaires and focus groups. Paul has a doctorate in adult education, and this background has been an important element in building our company's learning-centred approach to group process. The "we" in this book refers to Paul and myself.

Are You a Facilitator?

This handbook is designed for facilitators who have some experience working with groups and are interested in expanding their knowledge and expertise about how to make questions work well. This includes professional facilitators as well as teachers, trainers, community organizers, project leaders, lawyers, executives, professors, health care professionals, mediators, negotiators, human resources professionals, politicians, social workers, counselors, and managers. Many people do facilitation as a regular part of their work and yet don't think of themselves as professional facilitators – this resource is also for them.

Regardless of your role, the right questions for the right people at the right time are at the heart of healthy group process – a top priority in effective and dynamic facilitation.

Finding the Right Questions

Most facilitators spend considerable time looking for and thinking about a question for a particular moment in a particular situation with a particular group of people. Some questions work brilliantly with one group and not at all with another.

This handbook is designed to reduce the amount of effort and time required to find or develop questions that work. As with other resources in this series, the focus is on basic frameworks, on practical, proven, adaptable tools and a wealth of specific strategies and examples. This book is about questions that facilitators ask *during* sessions with participants. Questions to ask participants *before* sessions (e.g., needs assessments) and *after* sessions (e.g., evaluations) will be included in other ST Press publications. Please contact us by email at stpress@cyberus.ca for more information.

Dorothy Strachan

How to Use This Handbook

This handbook has two main parts.

Part I: How To Ask Questions explores some basics parameters for effective questioning.

> *Chapter 1, Making Questions Work,* focuses on how to make questions function effectively for you as a facilitator. It describes how to construct questions, types of questions and some dos and don'ts.

> *Chapter 2, Core Facilitation Values,* explores how your values guide the use of questions in support of healthy group process.

Part II: What to Ask When has six chapters and over 700 sample questions for situations where facilitators require specific types of questions to meet common challenges with groups. Although each chapter is designed to stand on its own, it is also interrelated with the others. For example, the values described in chapter 2 are at the heart of what makes the framework in chapter 4 work well, and the questions in chapter 5 on critical thinking may also be used to supplement the framework for addressing issues in chapter 6.

> *Chapter 3, Questions for Opening a Session,* provides tips on questions for the beginning of processes and a wide sample of questions to choose from.

> *Chapter 4, Questions for Enabling Action,* describes the "What – So What – Now What" framework, a three-step approach to outcomes-based facilitating.

> *Chapter 5, Questions for Thinking Critically,* helps participants reflect on how and why things are done the way they are, an important skill for complex problem solving in groups.

> *Chapter 6, Questions for Addressing Issues,* provides a systematic approach to six areas of inquiry related to issues analysis and management, a common element in many facilitated processes.

> *Chapter 7, Questions for Closing a Session,* includes a wide variety of options for challenges that facilitators face when concluding processes.

Each chapter includes a brief description of the challenge, guidelines for developing and using questions, lists of questions divided into focus areas, and suggestions for further reading. Space is provided for you to write down additional questions so that you can make this handbook into a personalized question bank.

Chapter 8, Questions for Specific Cases, includes responses to inquiries we receive from facilitators regarding challenges in specific cases.

By presenting what works for us, we hope that you will find some practical ideas and tools for asking people the right questions at the right time.

About Words

Several words that are used frequently throughout this book are explained below.

Client	The client is the person or group of persons with whom the process is developed and to whom the facilitator is accountable. The client may be a planning committee, an administrator, a Board of Directors, a manager or another responsible person or group.
Facilitator	A facilitator is someone who attends to group process. This includes professional facilitators as well as teachers, trainers, community organizers, project leaders, lawyers, executives, professors, health care professionals, mediators, negotiators, human resources professionals, politicians, social workers, counselors, and managers. Many people do facilitation as a regular part of their work and yet don't think of themselves as professional facilitators.
Group	Three or more people who want to accomplish something.
Group members	Participants in a group process; this phrase is used interchangeably with "participants".

Participants	People who are participating in a group process; this word is used interchangeably with "group members".
Plenary	When all members of an assembly are present; for example, when a number of small groups are together in a meeting of the whole group.
Probe	A follow-up question, variation or suggestion designed to clarify a response or to get more information in a specific area.
Process	A structured group experience; a process may happen in a variety of settings such as work sessions, workshops, meetings, conferences, round tables.
Session	A facilitated process that happens in a limited time period – a few hours, a day, a weekend, a week; may also be called a workshop, meeting or conference.

Please note that I have used gender-specific personal pronouns throughout the text to avoid using cumbersome his/her or he/she constructions.

Tell Us What You Think

Let us know what you think about this handbook (e.g., what works, what doesn't work, additional questions, suggestions for improvement) by e-mail at stpress@cyberus.ca. We appreciate your input and will acknowledge your suggestions.

Part I

How to Ask Questions

Chapter 1

Making Questions Work

Questions work when they contribute to the overall purpose and specific objectives of a process. They provide a format for gathering information, clarifying feelings and expectations, probing for examples, checking inferences and building consensus for decision making.

The right question is the one that works best at a particular moment in a particular situation with a particular group of people. Sometimes questions work brilliantly with one group and not at all with another.

When facilitating a group of chief executive officers who were developing a national strategy for business leadership, I asked participants to introduce themselves by answering the question, "What is an important learning you have had about organizational leadership in your working life?" They were to give their responses in the form of commandments.

Responses to this question were rich, concise and varied. They energized the group, focused the discussion, encouraged risk taking, generated new ideas and initiated the development of a national leadership vision.

Participants said things like:

- Enable people to mourn the past so that they can change. Build on the organization's legacy and traditions.

- Get the organization change-ready.

- Lead towards something, not away from something.

- Organizational leadership takes passion and big steps – leadership is not a spectator sport.

- Political and business leadership are not always going in the same direction.

Watching these responses work their magic with that group was a satisfying experience. During other introductions I have realized that the questions aren't focused enough or that they confront participants too much or too little. At other times, when writing a final report, we have discovered that a session might have been considerably more productive if we had just tweaked a few questions during small group discussions so that they directed participants more clearly towards a specific outcome.

When I consider that I have been looking for the right questions for many years, I am reassured by the fact that others in our field wrestle with similar challenges:

> *Skills as complex as questioning, listening, and response are learned step-by-step; mastery is a climb up a ladder, not a pole vault.*[1]

Constructing Questions

When thinking about what to ask participants, ask yourself the following three basic questions:

1. **What do I want to ask?**

   What information do we need to address our objectives (e.g., background information, facts, opinions, ideas, reflections, suggestions)?

2. **Why do I want to ask this?**

   How will the response to this question serve our objectives (e.g., problem analysis, challenging the status quo, prioritizing items, leading towards group decision making, clarifying attitudes, suggesting a hypothesis)?

3. **How might people respond?**

   What is a possible range of answers to this question? (What is the client's perspective? What other perspectives are there?)

Your responses to these three queries will clarify how the questions fit with your overall purpose and objectives.

Types of Questions

Facilitators use two main types of questions: closed and open. Each type produces different types of answers and has specific benefits and drawbacks in terms of group process.

Closed questions require **simple, specific answers** such as "yes" or "no". For example, "How long have you been working on this issue? How many people are on this team? When was this policy initially drafted? Whom do you call if you need support?"

Open questions can't be answered simply. They require some thought and a **developed answer.** For example, "How did you develop that perspective on this issue? What factors contributed to your success this year? Where is the current reorganization going to take the company?"

Closed questions

Closed questions are most appropriate in situations where there is a right and a wrong answer, or where one answer is better than another ("How many people are needed on this committee to ensure that it is effective and efficient?"). You can also use closed questions to get specific information from a participant, or in issues analysis, in problem solving or in enabling action ("If you decide to take this route, what is the first step?").

Closed questions are helpful when you want specific feedback about a situation ("Who supports this policy?") or when you want participants to edit a written statement such as a mission statement or a list of values. Closed questions also work when group members are prioritizing a list (e.g., selecting key directions in strategic planning).

Closed questions do have disadvantages in certain situations.[2] When you are trying to encourage group members to open up or to give a detailed response, closed questions that elicit brief factual responses may discourage candour and close down conversation.

Often, facilitators want to motivate participants to ask their own questions, both of themselves and of one another. Too many closed questions can discourage participants from reflecting on their situations and developing solutions in collaboration with other group members.

Closed questions may also shape the answers they request, as when group members try to anticipate what a facilitator wants to hear. For example, the question "How does this approach support your current vision?" makes the assumption that the approach is supportive, thereby shaping responses.

Another disadvantage can emerge if participants become dependent on a facilitator for asking leading questions that will steer participants to the "right" answer. In this situation, group members start to expect more from the facilitator and less from themselves. The facilitator has then abdicated her content-neutral position (see the discussion on Integrity in *Chapter 2, Core Facilitation Values*) and has become a problem solver or content expert. Similarly, a facilitator may ask questions in such a way that the group "discovers" a conclusion that the facilitator already holds. This Socratic teaching method may be appropriate in some learning situations but is inappropriate for content-neutral facilitators.

> *One strategy I use as a volunteer facilitator working in my content specialty area is to put on a red baseball hat labeled "content" when I want to ask a question or make a comment in relation to an issue. (A senior executive and volunteer facilitator)*

Situations are not always black and white. We often facilitate in areas where, because of our experience in a particular field, we know as much about the content as participants do. In these situations it is important to ask questions and provide content in a way that doesn't encourage dependency by participants. Dependency inhibits group maturation because members are not developing confidence in their abilities to solve their own problems.

Open questions

Open questions work well when you are trying to stimulate discussion and encourage critical reflection ("What approaches have you seen over the past year that have worked well in your company?") or when you want a group to engage in discussion leading towards consensus ("What are the supports and barriers in this situation? What strategies can you suggest to address this issue?")

You can also use open questions effectively when a group has reached a decision prematurely and needs to explore additional dimensions of an issue. ("What other issues did the research report mention that you should also consider?")

On the other hand, when you are coming to the end of a decision-making process and there seems to be tacit agreement on a conclusion, an open question can cause participants to re-examine needlessly an existing consensus.

Open questions invite people to explore their perspectives, opinions, thoughts and feelings about a subject. ("How do you think we can address this problem? What would you do if ...? How do you feel when you can't get to see your boss? Why do you think your employees refuse to follow your instructions after you've left for the day?")

There are disadvantages to using open questions. For example, if you have a limited amount of time for introductions, asking an open question extends your timelines and frustrates participants who are anxious to get into content. Participants may also become uneasy if you ask an open question that encourages discussion when you have only five minutes left to wrap up a session. They find it frustrating to be invited to participate in a stimulating interchange that will require them to abandon their agenda timelines.

In summary, constructing effective questions involves knowing what you want to ask, knowing why you want to ask it and understanding how your choice of closed or open questions can influence how people respond.

Guiding Principles

1

Six guiding principles for creating and asking questions can help facilitators to invite responses that support interesting and productive discussion:

1. Customize for context.

2. Create inviting questions.

3. Ask with sensitivity.

4. Accommodate risk.

5. Prepare participants for tough questions.

6. Ask follow-up questions.

1. Customize for context

There is no best way to facilitate, no model or approach that can be standardized to work in all or even most situations. Each group is unique and requires customized approaches for addressing specific challenges. This uniqueness creates an intriguing and complex dynamic for facilitators.

Context is the situation, circumstances and surrounding structures that weave together to frame a group's experience. Context consists of a variety of factors, including the purpose and objectives of a process, the literacy level of participants, the resources available for next steps and the nature, length and commitment of the sponsoring organization. Context also includes the history of the group, how members have worked together in the past, their interpersonal dynamics and their motives, personalities, learning styles, body language, decision-making preferences, power bases, political orientations, cultural heritage, academic backgrounds and familial backgrounds. It also involves participants' work and life experiences. Add to these dynamics the facilitator's own style, approach, background, body language and experience, and you have a complex mix!

To create effective questions that have meaning in a specific context, you need to

- know the process objectives and anticipated outcomes
- know the situation
- know the issues
- know the people
- know yourself.

The more you know about these five areas, the more focused your questions will be on the needs and interests of the participants and the client.

Comprehensive preparation is essential for a healthy process. Facilitators need to spend considerable time learning about a client, the organization, the situation and the participants by going through background documentation, interviewing people, summarizing main issues and researching recent publications. The final challenge – knowing yourself as a facilitator – is grounded in how you understand and apply your core values, as described in Chapter 2.

Questions that work well in one context may be completely inappropriate in another. You can successfully ask a group of senior managers what leadership skills they think are required to function well in their industry, but the same question is not likely to be as effective with inexperienced managers. A group of recreation leaders are more likely to respond well to introductory questions that have a "fun" orientation than are a group of stressed-out, time-pressed lawyers focused on task and efficiency.

Use the following checklist to customize your questions to suit a specific context:

- What are the objectives and expected outcomes for this process? How do they fit with the organization's mission, values and strategic directions?
- What is the context for this group?
- What makes this group unique (e.g., experience, cultural diversity, gender)?
- How can that uniqueness be embedded in the questions you ask?
- Given the experience and expertise of group members, what are they likely to be most comfortable discussing? Least comfortable discussing?

2. Create inviting questions

Interestingly, not all questions invite responses. Some questions discourage responses – for example, through the use of inappropriate humour, sarcasm or condescending put-downs. Ending a question with "Don't you agree?" or "Haven't you experienced this?" conveys too much authority to tempt a timid respondent to reply with anything but a positive response. Similarly, questions that begin with, "You mean you haven't heard of ...?" do not invite disclosure. Use the following tips to create questions that encourage participants to respond.

- Ensure that your questions are *relevant* (related to your overall purpose and specific objectives), *challenging* (stimulating people to think) and *honest* (not involving tricks or deceptions).

- Don't ask leading questions. The answer to a question should not be in the question – it should be in the participant.

- Facilitation is not teaching. Don't ask questions if you already know the answer. Good discussions provide ways for people to explore ideas. They are not tests of whether people know specific answers.

- Avoid "asking down". Sometimes facilitators need to define or explain a word or phrase in a question. If this is done incorrectly, it can be perceived as condescending. The following question talks down to participants: "How do you feel about your income tax – that is, the amount you have to pay the government on the money you take in during the year?" By inverting the term and the explanation, the question is much less condescending: "How do you feel about the amount you have to pay the government on the money you take in during the year – that is, your income tax?".³ Giving the explanation first and the definition second is a more conversational approach and avoids "asking down".

- Clear questions invite answers; questions with more than one interpretation invite anxiety. If you ask, "Have you ever used simultaneous translation?" participants may be reluctant to respond because they may not know whether you are talking about whisper translators or the entire technology of live translation, with microphones on tables and participants with receivers for the language of their choice.

If you ask, "Have you used individual receivers and microphones on tables for simultaneous translation?" participants understand exactly what you mean, that is, they hear the explanation first and the terminology second and are more likely to respond confidently.

- No one likes to appear foolish or ignorant. Avoid asking questions that will cause people to lose face in a group. To reduce the threat in challenging questions, use opening phrases such as, "Has anyone come across ...?" or "Have you ever run into ...?" or "Does anyone recall ...?" or "Has anyone had any experience with ... ?"

- Choose words carefully. Use words that all respondents will understand, avoiding special terminology, acronyms and words that have more than one meaning (e.g., "any" may mean "every", "some" or "only one"; "see" may mean "observe" or "visit a doctor or lawyer").[4]

- After you have asked a question, wait for the response. People need time to think. When you have asked a question and there is a silence, ask yourself, "Whose silence is it?" If participants are thinking about the answer, then it is their silence, and it is inappropriate to interrupt. If they are waiting for clarification, then it is the facilitator's silence, and she can speak into it. Experienced facilitators can "feel" a silence move from the group to the facilitator and vice versa.

- Think each question through before asking it. Rephrasing a question several times confuses the listener and discourages a response.

- Read and respond to the non-verbal messages or "vibes" in a group while you are asking a question. People can make it obvious through their body language when they think a question is appropriate or inappropriate.

3. Ask with sensitivity

Because questions have an emotional dimension, it is important to be sensitive to how you ask them. The effects of a question depend on tone, voice level, speed of delivery, facial expression, bodily stance and eye contact as well as content. You may pose questions on an emotional spectrum that ranges from distant (even hostile) formality to warm geniality. "What do you think?" can communicate many different meanings, depending on the questioner's inflection, emphasis and demeanor.[5]

Here are some suggestions for enhancing your sensitivity when asking questions.

- Use a bridge or linking sentence to introduce sensitive questions. For example, "Everyone in this room has been rejected on a promising cold call. Think about the last time this happened to you. What was your initial reaction when you realized that you were going to be turned down?"

- Ask permission to ask questions that are particularly sensitive: "May I ask how you decided to do it this way?" or "May I ask you a couple of questions about the situation in your office?"

- Use humour carefully. Generally speaking, if people laugh at the expense of others, then the humour isn't appropriate. Be particularly careful about sensitive topics, issues in "politically correct" areas, or "isms" such as racism and sexism.

- Be aware of your body language when asking questions:

  - Are you physically towering over a group of people who are feeling intimidated?

  - Do you cross your arms over your chest when you think a question is going to be resisted?

  - Do you ask questions when you are writing on a flip chart and your back is to the group?

  - Whom do you have eye contact with when you ask a question of an entire group?

  - Does your tone of voice sound as if you are inquiring or commanding?

- Use self-disclosure to express sensitivity. For example, in a bereavement support group: "I was really laid low by the death of my father. It was the first time in my life that I felt almost out of control. Has anyone else here felt that way?"

- Acknowledge the tension that people may feel when responding to sensitive questions: "Here's a question that may make some of you squirm a little, but it's important to our discussions."

4. Accommodate risk

Some questions carry a higher level of risk or threat than other questions. Generally speaking, the level of risk or threat goes up when group members feel that there is a "right" answer and they don't know what it is, or when the level of disclosure required to answer a question makes a participant feel uncomfortable.

The following suggestions can help facilitators address the risk factor in questioning.

- Normalize difficult questions and responses.

  When a regional manager is facilitating planning with a group of account managers who have not met quota, the question, "What prevented you from reaching quota this quarter?" can be risky, particularly if the regional manager is part of the discussion. Normalizing the challenges that account managers have faced can help reduce the risk in responding to this question. For example, the regional manager (in a facilitating role) could say, "Every one of us has felt the impact of company policy changes in our accounts this quarter and yet we haven't given up, and that's a good thing. We can learn a lot about what we have been through and how we might act in a similar situation by sharing our perspectives on this. So let's open up and talk candidly: What prevented us from reaching quota this quarter? I'll start off with something I think I could have managed better."

  Understanding and paying attention to the context for a process (see *1. Customize for context* earlier in this chapter) helps determine the level of risk in a question. In the previous example, the context makes it clear that this question is best asked by the regional manager, who is also a participant in the group.

1

- Before asking questions, be clear with group members about what is confidential (see the section *Clarify Confidentiality* in *Chapter 2, Core Facilitation Values*) and who will be informed about what was said or decided.

- Use low-risk questions that involve minimal challenge and require little self-disclosure before moving to higher risk questions involving more challenge and self-disclosure.

- Begin with questions that people are likely to be able to answer (e.g., personal opinions or ideas) so that you can build on their success before moving on to more difficult questions.

- Provide an opportunity to respond anonymously to questions through card sorting, multi-voting, sealed envelopes or diaries.

- Ask people to discuss risky questions in pairs, trios or small groups before bringing the discussion into plenary.

- Don't ask why when feelings run high.[6] In emotional situations, it is often difficult for a participant to state *why* he did something or to justify an action. He may be able to explain *how* something happened or *what* he did. But if he feels backed into a corner by a demand for a reason for his action, he may feel intimidated and just say the first thing that comes to mind or make something up. When you ask *why,* people often feel accused or blamed, which tends to initiate a defensive reaction.

   Asking why may also serve to take the experience away from the individual and transfer it to an authority figure – you as facilitator. Facilitators who ask "How did that happen?" or "What did you think about that?" are more likely to get accurate and truthful responses in difficult situations than those who ask *why*. You can avoid intimidating participants and enable them to provide more thoughtful answers if you "bye the why".

5. Prepare participants for tough questions

A general rule of thumb for tough questions is, "There should be no surprises." If you know you have a tough question coming up, provide some preparation time so that group members can think about what they want to say. Here are some options for preparing participants for challenging questions.

- Provide questions in the pre-meeting package.

  "During introductions we will be asking you to respond to the following two questions. Please come prepared with a one-minute response to each:

  a. When you think about Employee Assistance Programs over the past three years, what is the biggest challenge you have faced as a senior manager in Human Resources?

  b. What is your biggest challenge going to be over the next year?"

- Give participants a few minutes to review their background materials before answering. For example, "Review the pre-meeting paper and then jot down all the ideas that come to mind to describe your options for action." Then ask them to share their ideas with a partner and develop a list of three or four priorities. These two tasks help people to bridge into an answer.

- Plan the introduction of a tough question such that people will have time to consider it before answering. Consider the following example from a one-day planning session.

  Before the morning break: "After the break we will be listening to a presentation by Dr. Domuch. He will speak for an hour before lunch and then there will be a question-and-answer period after lunch. While you are listening to him, please take notes on how to do more with less, a question that we will be discussing after lunch."

  Before lunch: "As I mentioned earlier, we will be discussing the question of how to do more with less after lunch. You may want to keep this in the back of your mind over lunch or even discuss it while you are enjoying the flaming baked Alaska."

6. Ask follow-up questions

Follow-up questions can do much more than expand and clarify a response. They also can bring forward examples that stimulate empathy and understanding in group members. By asking follow-up questions, you are letting group members know that you are genuinely interested in their perspectives, thus building rapport and trust based on shared experiences. You are also enabling group development through self-disclosure.

Here are some suggestions for getting the most out of follow-up questions.

- When facilitating discussions, from time to time ask in an encouraging way if anyone has a different point of view. For example, "Let's hear a different perspective so that we don't get caught up in just one view," or "What are some other options here?"

- Ask for an example or an anecdote to clarify a response when someone provides you with a general answer to a question. Examples and anecdotes make a session more vibrant and immediate – they're the spice in the conversation, the hook that enables others to identify with a particular situation or experience.

- Probe for answers to your questions, asking for explanations and interpretations: "Tell me more," or "I'm not certain what you mean by that," or "Let's take this one a little further."

- The following eight categories of probes are hypothetical responses to the remark of the wealthy dowager princess: "I've had 33 lovers in 20 years." So startling a revelation requires some finesse in the probe-response.

Passive	"Hmmm ... I see ... "(Deadpan expression.)
Responsive	"Really? Thirty-three lovers? You seem to have led an interesting life ..." (Smile, nod, raised eyebrow, eye contact.)
Negatively responsive	"What a fickle woman you are!" (Frown, scowl, avoidance of eye contact.)

Developing	"Tell me more. Are you bragging or complaining? … Why so many? … What things do you most appreciate in a lover?"
Clarifying	"That's one and a half a year on the average; do you have affairs in sequence or concurrently? Do these men know about each other?"
Diverging	"And yet you claim to be in the forefront of the feminist movement. … Do you also know men merely as friends?"
Changing	"Okay, now tell me about your interest in Renoir paintings."
Involving	"Hey, Baby, who y'got in mind for number 34?"[7]

- Drawing people out through probes and follow-up questions sends the message, "Take your time; we are interested in what you are saying and want to hear your ideas."

- Interesting, dynamic and challenging discussions depend on clear ideas. Facilitators often need follow-up questions to get clarification about what someone is saying or to elicit additional information, as indicated in the following examples:

  - "Could you be more specific?"

  - "Tell me more about this. How did it start?"

  - "What suggestions can you offer based on these comments?"

  - "Can you say more about that?"

  - "Can you say that in another way?"

  - "Keep going …"

  - "What do you mean by the word '___'?"

  - "Please go on."

1

- "It looks as if people are keen to hear more. Would you expand a little on exactly how that happened?"

- "And then?"

- "What other options did you explore?"

- "Does anyone use that word in a different sense?"

- "Does this mean that …?"

- "How did you come to feel this way about …?"

- "To what extent has this fear/idea/suggestion become a reality?"

- "How do you feel that this situation came to be?"

- "What's your perspective/opinion/take on all this?"

- "Who else do you know in a similar situation?"

- "So, if I understand this correctly, you are asking …?"

- "And then what happened?"

- "Where else have you used this approach? How did it work?"

- "What else fits here?"

- "Who else has been in a similar situation?"

- "What comes to mind when you hear this?"

- "Would it be fair to say that you have a lot of confidence in that approach? Would it be fair to say that you are still questioning this approach?"

- "What do you suspect is going on here?"

- "Who sees something different in the report?"

- "What assumptions about human resources are you making with that response?"

- "What went through your mind when this was happening?"

- "What were your other choices in that situation?"

Next are some specific dos and don'ts for implementing these six guiding principles.

Dos and Don'ts

Asking questions is a skill acquired over time and with experience, and while we are acquiring experience, we often pick up habits – not all of which are helpful. The following tips are basic reminders for facilitators while they are acquiring experience.[8]

Instead of asking . . .	Try asking . . .	So that . . .
Do you understand the question? *or* Do you understand the task? *or* Who doesn't understand this?	Did I make the question clear? *or* Is that task clear or should I explain it a little further?	The responsibility for making the question or the task clear remains with the facilitator, not with the participant.
Who is responsible for supplying the flip charts?	Where can we get more flip chart paper?	The question invites rather than discourages a response.
Why are you feeling so upset?	How did the situation get to this point?	The focus is on correcting the problem rather than placing blame.
What are your options for ensuring that you are successful?	Let's brainstorm some options for addressing this problem. Be creative – in brainstorming there are no wrong answers.	The respondent is not made to feel defensive about answering the question. The respondent doesn't feel that she has to come up with all the right possibilities. The respondent isn't encouraged to develop an "either-or" answer.

1

Instead of asking . . .	Try asking . . .	So that . . .
You look pretty defensive, Gary – what's going on?	To what extent are things moving the way you expected, Gary?	You don't make an assumption about what Gary is feeling; instead you invite him to provide his own perspective.
We are almost finished, don't you think?	What do you think about how far we came this morning?	You are not requesting agreement. The authority implicit in "don't you think" implies that any disagreement must be mistaken – hardly a message to stimulate free inquiry.[9]
Why did you stop there instead of finishing the task?	What was happening for you when you stopped there?	The respondent does not feel pressured to develop a reason; instead he can simply describe what is happening for him.
What sort of data do you have to back up your opinion?	Tell me more. Has anyone researched this?	You are not putting the respondent in a defensive, weaker position.
Are things still pretty awful with your new supervisor?	How are things going now with your new supervisor?	You can avoid an assumption and direct the respondent to a constructive response.
Why are you so tired?	Your shoulders are drooping. What's up?	You don't prejudge how the person is feeling.

Instead of asking . . .	Try asking . . .	So that . . .
Let me be the devil's advocate. How can we avoid taking this route to solve this problem?	What other ways can you think of to solve this problem? *or* What about the point of view that …?	Group members don't lose sight of who believes what, and what has already been said. An opposing view is not perceived to be negative (e.g., belonging to the devil).
Define the word "strategic" for the purposes of this discussion.	How are you using the word "strategic" in this discussion?	The respondent feels less pressure to respond with the "right" answer. Asking for a description instead of a definition gives more permission to provide an individual perspective.
Do you agree or disagree?	What does that sound like to you? *or* Does this seem like a sensible approach? *or* How important is this issue to you? *or* Would you use this approach in your department?	You avoid forcing the respondent into an "either-or" answer. You can find out where respondents stand on a topic.
Do you think that having lobbyists in your planning session will taint the agreement building process?	Who has had experience facilitating lobbyists? How did the decision-making process go?	You can encourage a variety of opinions. You avoid asking questions that lead participants to a preconceived answer.

Instead of asking . . .	Try asking . . .	So that . . .
How might this change in the foreseeable future?	How might this situation with your human resources area change over the next six months?	You are specific when referring to a situation and a time period.
What are the big conflicts we are facing now in our team?	One of the first characteristics of well functioning teams is conflict. Today I want to discuss the ways we are successful in dealing with conflict among ourselves and where our challenges are. So let's begin. From your perspective, in what situations are we successful in addressing conflict?	You build a bridge or linking sentences when introducing sensitive questions. Participants feel support for being candid. You normalize what people are experiencing, i.e., they realize that their responses are not unusual.
Which of these objectives is the most important?	What is one question you want answered by the end of this session?	The focus is on participants' specific needs and interests. You acknowledge participants' questions as important.
She did a really good job on that one, don't you think?	Did her work meet your expectations?	You avoid persuasive tags at the end of questions; these tags can end up being statements disguised as questions.

Recommended Reading

Christensen, C. Roland, et al. *Education for Judgement: The Art of Discussion Leadership.* Boston, MA: Harvard University Press, 1991.

Cooper, Susan and Cathy Heenan. *Preparing, Designing, Leading Workshops: A Humanistic Approach.* Boston, MA: CBI Publishing Company, Inc., 1980.

Drucker, Peter F. *The Five Most Important Questions you will ever ask about your nonprofit organization.* San Francisco, CA: Jossey-Bass, 1993.

Eggleton, C. Harry, and Judy C. Rice. *The Fieldbook of Team Interventions.* Amherst, Maine: HRD Press, 1996.

Hart, Lois B. *Faultless Facilitation.* A Resource Guide for Group and Team Leaders. Amherst, MA: Human Resource Development Press, 1992.

Hunsaker, Phillip, and Anthony Alessandra. *The Art of Managing People.* New York, NY: Simon and Schuster, 1986.

Kayser, Thomas A. *Mining Group Gold.* How to Cash in on the Collaborative Brain Power of a Group. El Segundo, CA: Serif Publishing, 1990.

Sudman, Seymour, and Norman M. Bradburn. *Asking Questions.* A Practical Guide to Questionnaire Design. San Francisco, CA: Jossey-Bass, 1982.

1

Chapter 2

Core Facilitation Values

Core facilitation values are the deeply held beliefs that guide how you behave when facilitating. Values are statements of ideals, and it takes considerable effort over many years to make your values fully operational.

When I first started to facilitate professionally, I knew that it was important to be as objective as possible and that respect for participants was essential. I also knew that the more I could relax and be myself when working with groups, the better I felt about the whole process as well as the final product. However, it wasn't until I had spent time clarifying values with clients that I felt the need to be clear about my own core facilitation values.

Several facilitators have written about the importance of basing their practice on a set of core values. Chris Argyris and Roger Schwarz use the values of "valid information, free and informed choice and internal commitment".[10] John Heron talks about the need to respect "the autonomy and wholeness" of the learner.[11] Others emphasize the importance in group decision-making processes of core values such as full participation, mutual understanding, inclusive solutions and shared responsibility.[12] The values espoused by the International Association of Facilitators are participation, innovative form, social responsibility, global scope, inclusiveness and celebration.[13]

In our practice, three core values anchor how we facilitate and therefore also how we ask questions: integrity, mutual respect and authenticity. My role when facilitating is to model these values and enable their implementation while working with group members.

Integrity

As facilitators, our neutrality or objectivity is the heart of our integrity and our social contract with clients.

> *Content neutrality means not taking a position on the issues at hand; not having a position or a stake in the outcome. Process neutrality means not advocating for certain kinds of processes such as brainstorming. We found the power in the role of the facilitator was in becoming content neutral and a process advocate.*[14]

Integrity involves honesty, sincerity, freedom from moral corruption and conflict of interest, soundness of moral principle – in short, acting ethically. Working with others in groups is often complex, confusing and challenging. It is not easy to maintain a content-neutral perspective – and therefore your integrity – in the middle of discussions with participants or clients.

> *The facilitator's client is the entire group, not certain members. Consequently, the facilitator's interventions should not help certain members at the expense of others. Nor can the facilitator accept the views of one member as automatically representing those of other members.*[15]

Specific aspects of integrity in facilitation include confirming the roles of yourself and the chair, clarifying confidentiality, being sensitive to conflict of interest, avoiding collusion, asking questions ethically, avoiding intrusive questions and addressing imbalances in power and information.

Confirm roles of chair and facilitator

I am occasionally asked (as an external person) to facilitate a meeting along with a chairperson. This can happen for a number of reasons. For example, a not-for-profit organization might want to provide some profile to a volunteer chair during a session, a committee chair might have special content expertise in an area or a client might have some training or expertise in facilitation and wants to put it to use.

Co-facilitating with someone who has an interest in the outcome of a session may put your integrity as a facilitator at stake. In legal terms, the interested person is said to have a "reasonable expectation of bias". What, when, why and how questions are asked can have a significant impact on what, when, why and how decisions are made.

It is important to clarify and confirm your role as facilitator as well as the role of the chairperson. We usually have the chairperson introduce the meeting, give a brief history of what led up to the session, describe the motivation for calling people together and explain why there is an external facilitator. Then the chairperson hands the meeting over to the facilitator so that there is no confusion about who is managing the process. At this point two things happen: the chairperson becomes a full participant along with others involved in the session, and I confirm that my role as facilitator is to be content neutral and an advocate for a healthy and productive process.

Clarify confidentiality

Confidentiality is often an important part of integrity in facilitation. Confidentiality can be about what is communicated by participants during a session in response to questions. For example, are some topics off limits? It can also be about what people say after a session: What can be communicated about what was discussed or took place during a session? Confidentiality or secrecy clauses in contracts are common safeguards for clients who are concerned about job security, corporate espionage or secret policies.

Be clear and specific about the norm for confidentiality in a session, as in the following examples:

- "This meeting is off the record. We agree that there will be no report and that none of the parties involved will discuss any aspect of the meeting with others."
- "When asking questions of others, avoid confidential topics such as …"
- "Be candid and direct in your questions. We need open and thoughtful critical reflection to make this process work. Nothing is confidential."
- "Be open and caring with feedback. The report will disclose only key decisions, not discussions leading up to decisions. Discussions will remain confidential to members of this group."
- "No names will be attached to specific comments in the report."

Be sensitive to conflict of interest

If your client is thinking about hiring or promoting someone who is a participant in a session and asks you as facilitator to provide some observations on that person, you cannot take on that role and still maintain the trust of participants. They are counting on you to function in a neutral manner. If you accede to the client's request, you are in conflict of interest: you are both facilitating the group and evaluating a participant in terms of job worthiness.

When you are in conflict of interest, you jeopardize the integrity of your role as a facilitator. For example, you may end up asking questions that test whether the group member has the knowledge required to take on the job, rather than asking questions that support a healthy process leading towards the group's objectives.

Several years ago I took a course on negotiation that was being offered by members of a law firm from another city. Early in the course one of the facilitators said, "We are always on the look-out for new places to offer our course. Can you help us get in touch with the right people around here to see if there are any prospects?" I felt awkward hearing this question – I had paid for the course and wanted value for money, not to be solicited for future clients. Also, some of our company's law firm clients offered similar courses, and the question therefore seemed insensitive. I was uncomfortable hearing a sales pitch before I could even decide on the usefulness of the course. I felt that the facilitators were in conflict of interest.

Avoid collusion

Collusion is a secret agreement, whether stated or not, with a participant, client or co-facilitator. Collusion is inconsistent with the facilitator's role, because it requires the facilitator to withhold valid information and consequently prevents free and informed choice for certain group members. It places the interests of some group members or the client above the interests of the group as a whole.[16]

When a client asks a facilitator to ask the group a question because the client doesn't want the group to know that the question came from her, this is potential collusion. It is not uncommon for a group member to make a similar request: "Would you ask the group if they would like to … I don't want this question to come from me."

Ask questions ethically

Do you ever wonder why people tend to answer the questions that are asked in facilitated sessions? Occasionally, someone will say, "I choose not to answer that question now," but this is uncommon. Most often, people answer questions simply because they are asked – as if the facilitator-participant relationship includes an obligation to respond. For this reason, facilitators have an obligation to consider the ethics of asking questions.

Asking questions ethically is easy in simple situations – when you know what is morally right, when you understand what you want to ask and why you want to ask it, when the situation is clear and when little is at stake. However, facilitators rarely face simple situations. What is "right" is often complex and unclear and the stakes can be very high.

If your client or employer wants a specific result from a session and the group is leaning towards a different conclusion, how you ask a question can prejudice the outcome. For example, if you say, "The company is losing significant revenue because of employees coming in late. What do you think we should do?" the discussion is likely to start on a very different note than if you say, "Revenues are down 7% this quarter. What kinds of things are you noticing that could contribute to this loss?"

On occasion, I have experienced considerable pressure from clients who want a specific outcome from a session when that outcome does not reflect the experience of participants. Acting with integrity means asking the client up front what she would do if the group wanted an outcome that was different from what the client wanted. This question can open a discussion about values and how they translate into action. As facilitator, you need to feel comfortable using your values to guide both the group process and your own behaviour.

Avoid intrusive questions

Some questions are too intrusive for some participants. In such cases, participants can feel taken by surprise and unable to respond. Not everyone has the presence of mind to say, "I find that question intrusive and am not prepared to respond right now."

By reviewing your questions and approach with your client or planning committee, you can explore what types of questions might be considered intrusive for group members.

Address imbalances in power and information

In most groups, a disparity in power and information exists. It is easy to discount the power and influence of the facilitator and the potential impact of what may initially seem to be subtle decisions in relation to group process.

> *First, ethical decisions are unavoidable in discussion settings. Precisely because a session, event or workshop mirrors the fragile personal interactions of everyday life, human relationships and the associated ethical issues are continually at stake. Second, in such settings, absolute fairness is impossible, and trade-offs and compromises are inevitable. Someone is likely to be disadvantaged or displeased by almost every action; the facilitator's only hope is to establish a rough hierarchy of values, to monitor the personal and educational impact of resulting decisions, and when in doubt, to follow that priceless maxim, "Strive to do no harm."*[17]

As facilitators, our questioning practices can ensure that differences in power and information (e.g., confidential briefings and other data) are addressed openly. For example, how do you decide whom to ask questions or whom to call on during a session? Is there a pattern to who gets the best questions? Do you more often question people whose views are similar to yours than people whose views differ?

Several years ago in a heated exchange during a session with university faculty, a participant suggested that I was reluctant to call upon a particularly combative professor and that I had a responsibility to call on everyone equally. I learned a lot during that process as well as over the ensuing years by reflecting on that situation and whether I was acting with integrity.

How we ask questions, whom we ask, how frequently we ask them, when we ask them and for what purpose we ask them – all these decisions are wrapped up in our integrity as facilitators, simply because we have power, expertise and information that can influence the outcome of a process.

2

Mutual Respect

When asked to develop rules or norms for working together, most groups identify mutual respect as essential to a healthy process. When asked to describe what they mean by "mutual respect", they say things like "Everyone is important" or "Each of us has something to contribute or we wouldn't be here" or "Let's make sure that we really listen to each other and try to understand perspectives that are different from our own." These are all good descriptions of mutual respect.

Equity is an important aspect of mutual respect. More than the perception of fairness, it involves acting on a daily basis in a fair and unbiased way. There is a tendency to think of equality and equity as the same concept. Webster's defines "equal" as "of the same quantity, size, number, value, degree, intensity," and "having the same rights, privileges, abilities, rank, etc." Equity, on the other hand, is defined as "justice, impartiality; the giving or desiring to give each person their due; anything that is fair." Equality can be quantitatively measured, whereas equity requires a more qualitative assessment of what is fair and just.[18]

Facilitators can support equity by ensuring that various groups in a session have a voice, that is, that both dominant and less vocal groups are heard and respected. Questions that draw people out and that provide participants with an opportunity to clarify what they mean are important to supporting equity in sessions. A facilitator can say, "We're missing the back table – where do you stand in this discussion?" or "So far we have one view on the floor. What other perspectives are we missing here?"

An equitable process is based on inclusion; it respects the perspectives of everyone involved, even though they may not be reflected in a final decision. Become aware of questioning patterns you may be developing with a group – for example, asking more questions of people on one side of the room, or accepting that responses are appropriate before checking with other group members. Ensure that you offer everyone in the group equal opportunities to respond to questions. Equity and inclusion are important facets of mutual respect.

The following strategies can help you act on the value of mutual respect when asking questions.

Respect exchange times

Exchange time is the period between when one person finishes speaking and another person begins. Some people have extremely short exchange times. For example, when you see two people talking "on top of one another" during a conversation, there is little or no exchange time. Other people, whose style is more reflective, may need a much longer exchange time between when they are asked a question and when they feel prepared to respond. I have found, to my chagrin, that exchange times may also be culturally specific. I now make sure that I allow more time to facilitate when the group includes individuals or cultures with longer exchange times.

As a facilitator, it is important to respect a variety of exchange times and to encourage participants to do the same. Respect for exchange time encourages participants who are more reflective to participate in the discussion.

Be patient – whose silence is it?

Asking a question is like serving a tennis ball: You use the question (racquet) to put the discussion (ball) into play. Once you have asked the question, the silence in the room belongs to the respondents. Wait until they return the ball to you before you lob it back again.

With a little experience, facilitators can "feel" when a silence shifts back to them.

As a blind man, lifting a curtain, knows it is morning, I know this change.[19]

If you jump into a silence prematurely to rephrase a question or to ask a specific person to respond, you are reducing the amount of time that participants have to think about a question. In addition, you may be perceived by participants to be uncomfortable with silence, or to be unduly nervous, which can reduce your effectiveness with group members.

Encourage direct interaction

Dialogue among group members promotes a balanced and impartial climate and results in better decision making. Encourage group members both to ask and to respond to questions – without going through you as the facilitator – so that they can learn directly from each other and build respect for each other's competence.

Don't ask for facts

Adults participating in group discussions or decision-making processes do not usually need to be tested on facts. If you already know the answer, don't ask the question – just provide the answer. Adults find it disrespectful to be quizzed as if they were in grade school.

Sometimes when participants seem hesitant about responding to a question, I will say, "When I ask a question I am not looking for a 'right' or predetermined answer. I want to know what you think. This is not a test; it is a discussion."

Model mutual respect

It is easy to be disrespectful without intending to be. The following suggestions encourage mutual respect between facilitator and participants and among participants.

- Encourage participants to ask questions as they surface, except perhaps during formal presentations.

- Don't repeat unheard answers to questions; instead, encourage the respondent to repeat the answer more clearly.

- Whenever possible, avoid telling people that an answer will be given at another time: "We'll cover that tomorrow" or "That's not discussed until this afternoon." When the energy generates the question, the subject is on the table.

Authenticity

Authenticity is about being real or genuine. It is about avoiding self-deception, becoming more and more like yourself when working with others.

It is not about acting like someone else whom you admire, or telling jokes even though it's not your style. It is about the "struggle for mastery, not only of content and craft, but also of self." It is about learning to become so comfortable in your own skin that you view your own knowledge and expertise as instrumental to effective group process rather than as something to be displayed.[20]

Authenticity is a core value because it enables the facilitator to see the group more clearly, without the view being obscured by the facilitator's facade. Modeling authenticity also helps to elicit authentic responses from participants.

There is no best personality type for facilitators. The best personality type for you is your own.

Over the past 10 years we have found that participants in group processes are becoming increasingly concerned about authenticity. Robert Terry identifies six factors that contribute to this preoccupation:

1. a deep and undefined sense of disconnection from the institutions and people that we believe we should be connected with

2. information overload based on our technology-rich societies

3. an increasing mistrust of institutions, organizations and systems

4. the development of virtual realities, for example, through technology, spin control and disinformation

5. an increasing fragility of a shared sense of purpose

6. the rise of relativism, that is, people feel that they can never really know what is true or real or what is good or right.[21]

Given the presence of these factors, one constructive response a facilitator can make is to be authentic – to be genuine with participants and to ask the question that is often uppermost in their minds – "What is really going on here?" – in a skilled and caring way.

The following tips help facilitators to translate the value of authenticity into action through effective questioning skills.

Build group ownership for outcomes

Questions that work well help consolidate and strengthen the power of the group rather than the profile of the facilitator. If the answer to the question, "What is really going on here?" is that the facilitator is too focused on building her consulting practice, then both the process and the facilitator lack authenticity.

As participants in a group work together to ask and answer questions, solve problems or develop plans, they are building ownership for a product or anticipated outcome. If the facilitator plays too large a role in building the product, driving towards the outcome or influencing how it develops, group ownership suffers and participants may blame the facilitator if things don't work out the way they expect; or they may give the facilitator too much credit when things work out well.

> *Effective questioning is the engine that drives productive group process.*

Minimize self-deception

At the heart of authenticity is a refusal to engage in self-deception. Facilitators can avoid deceiving themselves about how well a process is going by asking themselves, workshop participants, planning committee members and other stakeholders how they are experiencing a session. Here are some approaches we have used:

• Be candid about your impressions of a session as a way to initiate a discussion about how things are going, for example, "This feels to me like we're getting bogged down in details; anyone else feel this way?"

- Support participants in the desire to disclose how they are feeling and what they are thinking about the process. Then, share a summary of that feedback with them as a starting point for making necessary changes.

- When appropriate, use humour (e.g., cartoons depicting difficult situations) to raise sensitive issues for discussion:

  Humor can be a powerful conduit to meaning. It is a way to convey otherwise unsayable truths about human existence. Like art, it reveals meaning by juxtaposing the obvious with the novel. Also like art, it frees the imagination through its ability to tear down boundaries and stereotypes.[22]

  Keep in mind that effective humour is not at someone else's expense.

- Ask participants (sensitively) about unclear messages or possible self-deception. For example, "It sounds as if there might be a statement behind your question – do you want to raise another issue?" Your question should be a gentle challenge to support disclosure; it should not intimidate or irritate participants.

Be clear about intentions

Sometimes when observing a group, I have seen the tone shift positively when members have realized that the facilitator is well intentioned, neutral and focused on clear outcomes and wants to ensure that their experience is positive and productive. That shift happens when you are clear about your intentions and participants encounter your authenticity – when they see that you are being yourself in a difficult situation.

Once this shift happens, you can even make an error in judgement and the group will still support you because they can see your positive intentions. They respect your sincerity.

I find that being transparent about my relationship with a client can help create a positive tone. I may say, "I have met with _____ and we have been clear that there is no predetermined outcome for this session. My role is to ensure a healthy process. If I stray into content, please let me know right away." Transparency about intentions supports authenticity.

Acknowledge problems

Being authentic also means acknowledging when things aren't going well. For example,

- "Looks like this activity isn't working very well. What's happening?"

- "Let's change the approach here so that we are more focused on our objectives. How could we make this more meaningful for everyone?"

- "You look confused. How about if I try to give those instructions more clearly?"

Closing Thoughts: Leaning on Values

One of my first contracts as a facilitator in the '70s was in high performance sport with Canada's National Coaching Certification Program (NCCP). Before the NCCP's inception, most coaches emulated other successful coaches. For example, if a successful Olympic swimming coach taught athletes to do the front crawl with a flat, closed hand moving through an S-curve underwater, then there would be a large number of coaches emulating that practice, often without understanding why, that is, the bio-mechanical principles involved. Because these coaches didn't understand stroke mechanics, they couldn't correct individual problems with any specificity.

Although there is much to learn from watching others, imitating others also means imitating their mistakes. There is no single best way to facilitate, no optimal personality to imitate, no magic answer for how to support healthy group process and the achievement of objectives. People facilitate best when they know and act on their core values and are skilled and well prepared.

Three core values are easy to remember and can support me when I am feeling unsure about what may be happening with a group. I count on the fact that if I am acting with integrity, mutual respect and authenticity, even the most challenging situations will yield good results.

Recommended Reading

Brockett, Ralph G., Ed. *Ethical Issues in Adult Education.* New York, NY: Teachers College Press, 1988.

Dalla Costa, John. *The Ethical Imperative: Why Moral Leadership is Good Business.* Toronto, ON: HarperCollins, 1998.

Halberstam, Joshua. *Everyday Ethics:* Inspired Solutions to Real-Life Dilemmas. New York, NY: Penguin Books, 1993.

Lewis, Hunter. *A Question of Values: Six Ways We Make the Personal Choices That Shape Our Lives.* New York, NY: HarperCollins, 1991.

Schwarz, Roger M. *The Skilled Facilitator.* San Francisco, CA: Jossey-Bass, 1994.

Strachan, Dorothy, and Paul Tomlinson. *Gender Equity in Coaching.* Ottawa, ON: Coaching Association of Canada, 1996.

2

Part I – In Summary

Asking questions effectively is both a science and an art. The science part happens through research focused on skill development in such disciplines as psychology, sociology, group process and facilitation. The art part comes when the facilitator trusts the synergy of her experience and her intuition to guide questioning.

The final goal for facilitators is what Aristotle called praxis – theory into action – science and art combined. With good praxis, we are so comfortable with both the research and the intuition that they are one in how we act.

Part II of this handbook focuses on praxis.

Part II

What To Ask When

Introduction

Part II provides guidelines and examples for addressing five common facilitation challenges with groups: opening a session, enabling action, thinking critically, addressing issues and closing a session. The last chapter suggests sample questions for specific cases.

Each of the first five chapters of Part II includes a brief description of the challenge, guidelines for developing and using questions, lists of questions divided into focus areas, and suggestions for further reading. Space is provided for you to write down additional questions, so that you can make this handbook into a personalized question bank.

The purpose of Part II is to provide ideas for questions that will make your sessions dynamic, focused, participatory and productive. These questions are meant to stimulate you in developing your own inquiries. They can be used in a variety of situations, including large conferences where people share information at tables, in strategic and sales account planning sessions, public policy forums, board meetings, coach-athlete meetings, team development workshops and so on. The questions can also be used in a variety of formats: participants can respond verbally or record their responses on flipcharts; people can work in small groups to answer questions as part of a focused discussion; questions may be part of organized introductions or may be asked informally during registration.

Adapt the questions to suit your specific situation – for people who have never met before, for those who work together on a day-to-day basis or for those who meet quarterly or semi-annually. Individual questions may be appropriate for more than one section. For example, you will find questions in "Thinking Critically" that will also fit under "Addressing Issues".

> *How does each question contribute to the overall purpose and specific outcomes of your process?*

Chapter 3

Questions for Opening a Session

When opening sessions, meetings and workshops, the main challenge for facilitators is to create a positive climate that supports participants in achieving their objectives. Opening questions help to initiate the group development process and to focus participants on content and outcomes.

The cliché "You only get one chance to make a first impression" certainly holds true for group process. How you structure what people say during the opening part of a session can have a significant impact on how comfortable participants feel about taking part in the process, how confident they feel with you as a facilitator, and how willing they are to disclose and discuss issues and concerns.

After describing overall guidelines for opening questions, specific questions are provided for three areas:

1. getting to know one another – personal information and work experience

2. setting group norms – ground rules and ownership

3. clarifying expectations – hopes and concerns, and objectives and outcomes.

Guidelines for Opening Questions

Opening questions serve a session in many ways. Use the blank space at the right-hand side of the page to check off the guidelines that you want to remember for openings.

a. Because introductions contribute to healthy group development, it is important to provide an opportunity for people to get to know one another, set some norms, build ownership and clarify expectations. However, opening sessions vary in terms of the amount of time available for introductions. Sometimes (e.g., for a three-hour meeting involving 40 people), there is little or no time for introductions other than a statement of name, location and how a person is involved with a particular project.

Pace your opening questions so that the timing is right, given the length of the overall session (e.g., 10 minutes for introductions for a three-hour session or 45 minutes for introductions for an eight-hour session or 2 hours for introductions for a three-day session). _____

b. Relate your opening questions directly to session outcomes so that participants can see the link between the questions and their productivity during the process. This builds ownership for expected outcomes. For example, "In light of our objectives, what would make you feel really good about this meeting?" _____

c. Set questions that support each participant in making a positive initial impression: "What was your first positive experience earning money?" _____

d. Play to participants' strengths by creating opening questions that enable all participants to feel included as legitimate members of the group: "Which part of this project interests you the most? Why?" _____

e. Record the responses to one or two questions (e.g., write them on flip charts) so that you can revisit them at some later point in the process. _____

3

f.   Consider risk carefully. Some meetings and workshops need to begin with low-risk, non-threatening questions that enable people to share personal information and build rapport in a comfortable setting. Other meetings and workshops need to begin with higher risk questions that enable disclosure on issues and rapidly drive the agenda towards action. Consciously design an appropriate degree of risk in your opening questions.   _____

g.   Select questions that provide an opportunity for participants to disclose their concerns, anxieties and potential areas of disagreement in a non-threatening, safe and relatively low-anxiety setting: "What is one hope or one concern you have in relation to this meeting?"   _____

h.   Use questions that enable participants to make the transition from their day-to-day reality into the reality of the session: "What did you have to do to clear your desk and make it here today?"   _____

i.   Have one question that assists participants in establishing support networks that will sustain them after the session is over: "What is one thing you would like to learn from someone else at this session?"   _____

j.   Avoid icebreakers in warm climates. You need icebreakers when there is ice, that is, a hard, cold surface that requires some melting or breaking to smooth your passage to wherever you are going.

You don't need icebreakers when there is no ice – when people in the group are comfortable with one another or when they can see where they are going and have the confidence to figure out how to get there.

Participants can resent get-to-know-you games and other warm-up techniques for meetings or workshops when they serve no useful purpose – when they already know one other or when they can't make an obvious link between the game and the objectives of the session. In these cases, instead of a game, consider asking a question with some risk in it that pushes people to think about the issues to be discussed.   _____

3

k. Ask questions about experiences that are related directly to your specific objectives. Do not encourage long descriptions of academic credentials, previous job experience or publishing credits. For example, "What is one learning experience you have had in the past few years that relates to this issue? Describe what you learned in a single short sentence." _____

l. Use the final question to provide a link into the next part of the agenda: "What is one thing you want to get out of this session that relates directly to what you are doing now at work?" _____

3

Getting to Know One Another

When a group is forming,[23] participants benefit from a supportive structure. They need to know that the session is well organized, that someone is responsible for getting things moving, that there is an agenda and objectives and that they are valued for what they can contribute to the process.

Whether you are enabling participants to meet people for the first time or starting a team development workshop with people who know each other fairly well, effective questions can help participants with the motivation and ownership required to work with others and get a job done.

The following questions focus on people learning about one another by sharing personal information and work experience. Adapt the questions depending on whether people are strangers or already know one another, or if you have some combination of both in the group.

Focus: Sharing personal information

- "What would you like to know about one another?"

    Tip: Brainstorm some suggestions with the entire group (three to five minutes) and then make up a list of two or three questions for each person to consider.

- "What kinds of people make a positive first impression on you?"

- "Think about 'first impressions'. What two words to describe yourself do you want people to think when they meet you for the first time?"

- "What is a nickname you had as a child? How did you get it?"

- "What is one non-work interest or activity of yours that most people here may not know?"

  Tip: This works well both with group members who know each other and with those who don't. How you ask this question (verbally and non-verbally) determines how safe people feel in responding. Try using humour and give an example. We have had responses that range from spider collections to reading romance novels.

- "Most of us climb a number of 'mountains' in our lives. What is one mountain you climbed, and what did you learn from that experience?"

- "What is a major change you have made at some point in your life that, overall, has had positive results? What is a major change you have initiated that, overall, has had less-than-positive results?"

- "Where are you from? Tell us one interesting fact about your home town."

  Variation: Put a plasticized map on the wall and provide participants with coloured dots to place on their geographical location. Different colours can represent different reasons for participation, such as a red dot for a national perspective and a blue dot for a regional perspective.

- "If you could start a new political party, what would it be called and why?"

- "If you could change one thing about your education that would prepare you better to work with our company, what would that be?"

  Tip: By starting a question with "If you could …," you open up possibilities for people.

- "In adult education terms, an 'aha' is a significant learning experience. What is one 'aha' you have had about working in this organization? Please state your 'aha' in a single sentence."

- "What interests do you have outside of work that contribute to your effectiveness at work?"

- "What motivated you to work as a teenager? What motivates you to work now?"

> *Barbara Walters once revealed to the* New York Times *her five "foolproof" questions for the over-interviewed:*
>
> - *"If you were recuperating in a hospital, who would you want in the bed next to you, excluding relatives?"*
> - *"What was your first job?"*
> - *"When was the last time you cried?"*
> - *"Who was the first person you ever loved?"*
> - *"What has given you the most pleasure in the last year?"*[24]

- "In a single sentence, describe one thing in your life that you are thankful for."

    Tip: By limiting people to a single sentence you encourage them to focus their thoughts.

- "What is one thing in your life that you are looking forward to over the next year or so?"

- "Complete the following sentence: 'My ultimate destiny is to ...'"

- "Describe a fairly ordinary experience you have had that has significant meaning for you. What meaning did you take from this experience?"

- "What gift, experience or unique contribution do you bring to this project?"

More Questions on Sharing Personal Information:

Focus: Work experience

The word "work" is used here in its most general sense, that is, paid, volunteer, in the home – however the participant views it.

- "What is one memory you have of your work experience that you enjoy revisiting? What is one memory you have of your work experience that you don't enjoy at all?"

- "Describe your first experience with earning money."

   Tip: This question can be useful when opening a planning session for sales people.

- "When it comes to managing, who was your most important teacher? What is one important thing you learned from that teacher?"

   Tip: This question works well with a variety of substitutions for the word "managing," such as "selling", "communication" or" planning".

- "How did you make your first dollar?"

   Tip: Vary this question to suit your objectives; for example, "What are the first words that come to mind to describe your initial experience as a trainer in conflict management?" or "What was your first memorable experience as a manager?"

- "If you could have any job you wanted in any type of company anywhere in the world, what would that be?"

- "How does your organization show that it cares about its employees?"

- "What three things do you do most in a typical day on your job? Be specific so that we know exactly what it is that you do."

- "What is it about your organization and the work you do that you appreciate the most? What is it about your organization and the work you do that causes you the most irritation?"

- "What aspects of your work in policy development are most satisfying? What aspects are most frustrating?"

  Variation: Substitute other areas of work for "policy development".

- "How do you show the people you supervise that you care for them?"

- "What was your primary motivation in coming to work for this organization? To what extent has this motivation been fulfilled?"

- "What is your most important contribution to this team? What do you get from this team?"

- "What do you do to escape from the pressures you experience at work?"

- "Most people want to work in an environment where they feel happy about what they do. When do you feel happy at work?"

- "What is one stereotype that you have heard about people in our industry? In what sense do you agree or disagree with this stereotype?"

- "What do you find most rewarding about your involvement in this area? What do you find most challenging about your involvement in this area?"

- "How have you been involved with this project up to now?"

- "What other group processes (e.g., planning, training, team development) have you been involved with that are similar to this one?"

  Probe: "What did you learn from these processes?"

More Questions on Work Experience:

Setting Group Norms

The commitment of participants to the outcome of a process builds with mutual support for shared norms or ground rules, the opportunities they have to air or discuss their points of view with one another and the sense they have of contributing to outcomes.

Questions in this section focus on ground rules and building ownership for outcomes.

Focus: Ground rules

- "What is a watchword for this meeting that will help make it successful?"

- "What is one really helpful thing that you learned about working with others that has stayed with you? How could that learning be useful for how we work together during this meeting?"

- "What did you learn about being a member of a group or a team while you were growing up?"

- "What is one rule you learned in grade school that you wish everyone would follow during sessions like these?"

  Tip: Thinking about specific aspects of their past focuses participants on hindsight learnings and the need to apply them in the present.

- "What are the characteristics of an effective meeting? How can we ensure that our meeting has these characteristics?"

- "What is one thing that we can do to support each other in achieving our objectives?"

- "We have a wide range of participants in this session. Some are actively advocating a point of view and others are inquiring about perspectives on this issue. What are some guidelines that will help us balance advocacy and inquiry throughout this workshop?"

- "What are the top two things you teach (or would teach) your children about conflict management?"

  Tip: Avoid asking questions such as "How did you learn about conflict while you were growing up?" as this may surface painful memories (e.g., abuse, parental conflict) for participants.

- "What are some boundaries that we can set to keep us focused on our specific task and objectives and prevent us from trying to be all things to all people?"

- "Think about what we want to get accomplished through this session. Then think about yourself and others participating in this session. What are three or four basic 'rules of the road' or guidelines for working together that would support us in being successful as we work together?"

  Suggestion: You may want to give a couple of examples, such as coming back from the breaks on time, putting beepers on 'vibration' setting and turning off cellphones during sessions.

- "What are all the ways that people can sabotage sessions like this one? Think about your school years between the ages of about 13 and 17 and make a list of all the things you used to do (or saw others do) that would sabotage the possibility of a successful learning (meeting) experience."

  Suggestion: Turn this sabotage list into a set of norms by discussing the opposites.

- "What will this group look like at the end of its task when people are really working well together?"

- "What is one thing you do not want to see happen in this session?"

- "We have a full agenda and some specific outcomes to achieve. I see a key part of my facilitator role as creating a positive and productive context – keeping us on time and on topic. Are you comfortable with this?"

- "Given your experience with this group, what is one thing that everyone could do at this meeting to ensure its success?"

- "What is a ground rule that you have had at other meetings that you would like (or not like) to have for this meeting?"

More Questions on Ground Rules:

3

Focus: Building ownership

- "What motivates you to do a good job for this organization? What would motivate you to make a 150% commitment to this workshop process?"

- "If you could change one thing about how this board functions, what would it be?"

    Variations: "If you could change one thing about ... how we work together, how we do our work, how feedback is given, how we are paid, etc."

- "You have been asked to design a welcome mat for people coming into this workshop room. What would you put on your welcome mat?"

- "What is one thing you have learned about this area since we met last?"

- "Describe a proud moment in relation to your work on this issue."

- "How do you evaluate how successful a meeting is?"

- "What are you certain about with respect to being a member of this group? What are you uncertain about with respect to being a member of this group?"

- "What do you think is unique about this group? "

    Variation: This question can be adapted by substituting a different word for "unique".

- "What two values do you have that you think most people in this group share? What two values do you have that you think some people in this group may not share?"

- "What needs to happen during this process to ensure that you are fully committed to the outcomes?"

    Variation: Change the last part of this question.

- "What would make you feel really good about this process?"

- "How do you see your role in this group?"

- "What do you think needs to happen at this meeting to ensure its success?"

More Questions on Building Ownership:

3

Clarifying Expectations

It takes time to clarify process objectives and outcomes. No matter how clear the purpose of a session may seem to you as facilitator, participants often interpret that purpose in a variety of ways. The following opening questions help to clarify participant expectations by discussing hopes and concerns and confirming objectives and outcomes.

Focus: Hopes and concerns

- "What is one hope you have for this session? What is one concern you have in relation to this session?"

  Tip: Be clear about what you mean by a hope and a concern. Questions that ask for opposites tend to get similar responses, for example, "This is my hope and my concern is the opposite of that."

- "What motivates you to be involved in this project?"

- "What is one question you would like answered by the end of the day today?"

  Tip: Record and post participants' questions so that you can check them off as they are answered during the session.

- "Which parts of this process interest you the most? Which parts are relatively uninteresting to you?"

- "This committee has been in place now for three years. From your perspective, what has the committee accomplished? In what areas has the committee been less successful?"

- "Think about this project as a potential investment. What aspects of the project would encourage you to invest in it?"

- "What excites you about this realignment process? What causes you concern?"

More Questions on Hopes and Concerns:

3

Focus: Objectives and outcomes

- "Given your position in the organization, what changes would you like to see that would also benefit the organization as a whole?"

- "Where do you like to provide some leadership on projects like this one?"

- "Please review the objectives posted on the wall. Do these seem realistic and complete to you? If not, suggest changes."

  Tip: Confirming objectives builds ownership for the process and outcomes of a session.

  Probe: "The fourth objective refers to 'shared interests and problems of researchers in your field'. Based on your experience, what interests and problems would you like to see addressed at this workshop?"

- "Outcomes for this session that will make it successful for me are ..."

- "In a single, brief sentence, in your own words and from your perspective, answer the question, 'Why are we here?' "

- "What are you expecting from others during this session? What do you think they are expecting of you? What are you expecting of yourself?"

- "From your perspective, what is the most important outcome this project will achieve?"

- "What needs to happen to make this workshop successful from your perspective?"

  Variation: "What would success look like, feel like, to you?"

- "This committee has been in place now for three years. What would you like to see the committee accomplish over the next three years?"

- "As a new department is formed from merging your two work units, what aspects of how work was done in your unit would you like to make sure is kept in the new department? What aspects would you like to change?"

    Variation: This question on what to keep and what to change can be adapted to various situations by substituting other phrases for the underlined words.

- "Think about the end of this process. What legacy would you like to see in place for your organization?"

More Questions on Objectives and Outcomes:

3

Recommended Reading

Berne, Eric. *What do you say after you say hello?* New York, NY: Bantam Books, 1972.

McKay, Matthew, Ph.D., Martha Davis, Ph.D., Patrick Fanning. *Messages: The Communications Skills Book*. Oakland, CA: New Harbinger Publication, 1983.

Porter, Lawrence and Bernard Mohr. *Reading Book for Human Relations Training,* Eighth edition. Alexandria, VA: NTL Institute, 2001.

Stanfield, R. Brian, ed. *The Art of Focused Conversation*. Toronto, ON: New Society Publishers, 2000.

3

Chapter 4

Questions for Enabling Action

Facilitated discussions are directed towards clear and specific outcomes. Whether the purpose of a group is to do strategic planning, team development, account planning, implement a project, write a policy, develop best practices or revise a production schedule, action is required of the individuals involved, as well as for various subgroups and for the larger organization or community.

By using the *"What? – So What? – Now What?"* framework to guide questioning and stimulate discussion, facilitators can play a key role in keeping people on track and enabling action.

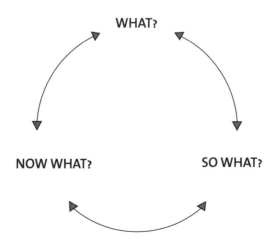

As the diagram suggests, this action framework has three main steps. Usually the facilitator describes the discussion topic or task (content) clearly in terms of objectives: "Our purpose here is to review and finalize the mission. Let's take a look at the summary of focus group results and see what they tell us about our mission statement."

1. A **notice** question from the **What?** category (on the following pages) leads participants to make some observations about this content.

   "What stands out for you about our mission statement as a result of reading this report?"

2. A **meaning** question from the **So What?** category asks participants to consider or reflect on how their observations fit with their current situation and values.

   "What do these observations tell us about the appropriateness of our mission statement and how it fits with our organizational values?"

3. An **application** question from the **Now What?** category asks participants to think about possible action steps or behaviour change.

   "How do you want to change the mission statement? Which key words or phrases should be changed?"

The *"What? – So What? – Now What?"* framework is handy and easy to remember. As the previous diagram illustrates, you can use these three questions to frame a specific task or discussion and enable it to move towards action. This framework also appeals to a variety of learning styles:[25] The people who like to observe will find their strengths in the notice ("What?") questions; those who are adept at reflection and abstract conceptualizing will enjoy the meaning ("So What?") questions; those who are skilled at taking action will find their niche in talking about applications ("Now What?").

> *Knowledge is produced in response to questions. And new knowledge results from the asking of questions. ... Once you have learned how to ask questions – relevant and appropriate and substantial questions – you have learned how to learn and no one can keep you from learning whatever you want or need to know.*[26]

4

Guidelines for Using the *"What? – So What? – Now What?"* Framework

Use the blank space at the right-hand side of the page to check off the guidelines that you would like to emphasize more.

a.   Start with where the group is: In some discussions participants begin with "So What?" questions and then go back to "What?" questions before moving into "Now What?" The questions are interdependent: remember to go through all three questions using the order that makes sense for a particular situation.   _____

b.   Learning styles have an impact on your success in using this framework. If you have a lot of participants whose learning styles lean towards taking action, they may want to skip the "So What?" questions or spend less time on them than people whose learning styles lean more toward reflection and generalization. Pace your questions to suit your group, ensuring that you spend an adequate amount of time in each of the areas on the framework, but not so much that you bore or distract people who have strengths in different learning styles.   _____

> *The effective facilitator is situationally responsive. He or she guides any particular group of participants to find learning that is meaningful and testable for them, regardless of whether it fits with the author's or facilitator's conceptual scheme. In other words, the process is trusted to unfold and evolve. The ideal facilitator does not lead the participants to conclusions but rather stimulates insights and then follows what emerges from the participants.*[27]

c.   If a discussion gets bogged down or there is too much silence, it is often because the discussion is "stuck" in an inappropriate part of the framework. For example, you may have asked a "Now What?" question about applying information provided in a video or a presentation at a time when the participants were just starting to notice things ("What?") about it. Or you may be facilitating the values clarification part of a strategic planning meeting with a group that includes a lot of people who are impatient about getting to the action steps. Pace the framework to suit the group. _____

d.   When working through the framework, normalize the variety of perspectives in a group as well as the potential for conflict. For example, "There are usually more than one or two perspectives on this issue: What other points of view can we raise here?" or "Conflicting perspectives are what make discussions like this one interesting. Who has another view?" _____

e.   The "So What?" part of the framework asks people for their opinions about how things fit together. Questions on this part of the framework that begin with "how" are usually less intimidating than those that begin with "why". A "how" or "what" question asks for a description, whereas a "why" question tends to ask for a reason or explanation. Many participants don't like to explain their actions or give reasons in a group. If required to do so, they can become defensive and either stay silent or make up what they perceive to be an expected response.

> *A gymnastics coach asked an athlete, "Why did you slow down at the big turn?" The athlete looked down and said nothing. When I asked her later about her lack of response, she said, "No matter what I said, I knew it would be wrong." When I asked the athlete (in a non-threatening tone), "What were you thinking about as you came up to the big turn?" she responded, "My line of approach seemed off and I wasn't sure I could complete that landing safely." (A parent)*

Avoid asking why when feelings run high. _____

f.   Setting a clear purpose and objectives at the front end of the framework is essential to the formulation of *"What? – So What? – Now What?"* questions. _____

"What?" – The Notice Questions: Observations

"What?" questions are important because they raise awareness – they ask participants what they think and feel about something.

> *Traditional aboriginal teachings seem to suggest that people will always have different perceptions of what has taken place between them. The issue, then, is not so much the search for "truth" but the search for – and the honouring of – the different perspectives we all maintain. Truth, within this understanding, has to do with the truth about each person's reaction to and sense of involvement with the events in question, for that is what is truly real to them.*[28]

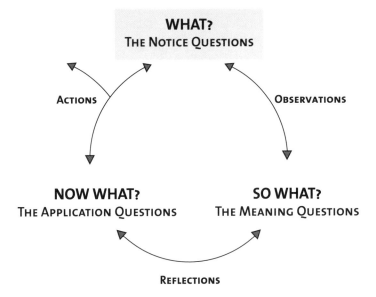

Following are sample "What?" questions for use in the framework. These questions could follow a presentation, video, report review, discussion or structured activity.

- "What did you notice?"

- "What stood out for you?"

- "What happened there?"

- "Any surprises here?"

- "So – what's your gut reaction to this approach?"

  Tip: This question could be used after a controversial or stimulating speaker. You could replace "gut reaction" with other phrases such as "initial response" or "intuitive response."

- "Has anyone else has had a similar experience?"

- "What did you observe when you did that?"

- "What is another way to say this?"

- "What caught your eye in this report?"

- "In buzz groups of three, share your impressions of this presentation and come up with two questions for the speaker."

- "What general feeling does this video leave you with?"

- "What are the first three words that come to mind after seeing that film?"

- "What struck you about that?"

  In order to grow in awareness, the individual may have to stop the action, pause and centre directly on himself. What am I feeling at this moment? What is happening within me right now? What is my mood? Do I feel tensions in my body? If I listen carefully, can I actively be in touch with the source of my discontent? What do I want? What do I prefer? How many different levels of awareness can I reach when I am alone? Can I describe each feeling? What thoughts and feelings stand out? Concentrated attention and focusing are initial steps through which awareness develops.[29]

- "How did that feel?"

  Probe: "Who had a similar reaction when listening to this speaker? Who had a different reaction?"

- "What parts of this presentation do you relate to most?"

- "What is happening here?"

- "What kinds of feelings did you experience while watching this video?"

- "Do you see any patterns here?"

- "What did you hear that you don't already know? What did you hear that you need to hear again?"

- "How involved were you in this presentation? Were you riveted, or thinking about things in the office, or doing a grocery list?"

- "Have you ever experienced anything similar to this?"

  Probe: "What are some examples of similarities (differences)?"

- "What potential problems or challenges jump out at you in this report (approach, plan)?"

More "What?" (Notice) Questions:

_____

_____

_____

_____

_____

4

"So What?" – The Meaning Questions: Reflections

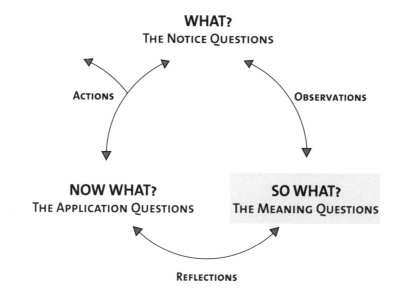

The following "So What?" questions are grouped into three focus areas: overall meaning and fit, organizations and the nature of work, and personal development.

Focus: Meaning and fit

- "Does this make sense to you? In what way?"

- "What key points can we pull from this presentation?"

- "How does what we are discussing here fit with our mission (our department's purpose, our unit's key objectives)?"

- "How does this compare with what you expected?"

- "What has been done about these problems so far?"

- "What is your dream for this area in 10 years' time?"

- "What did you learn or re-learn from this discussion?"

- "What parts of this report or presentation are relevant to your organization?"

- "Can you recognize your situation here?"

- "Why does this feel so important to you?"

- "How does today's session relate to our last meeting?"

- "Where's the meat in all this?"

- "How do you account for that happening in that situation?"

- "Is this what you thought might happen?"

- "What concerns does this raise for you?"

- "What did you learn or re-learn?"

- "What does all this mean to you?"

- "What was significant for you in this approach? Why?"

- "How does this relate to what we were talking about in the last session?"

- "What do you notice about the characteristics of your group in relation to the recommendations in the report?"

- "Does this video make any assumptions about race (or gender, age, class, religion) that have an impact on its conclusions?"

- "How are contradictions and dilemmas addressed in this report?"

- "What options were available in this situation that were not discussed?"

  Probe: "Why do you think these options were not put on the table?"

- "Does this approach (film, report) remind you of anything in your past experience?"

- "Would you hire this speaker (use this video, hold this discussion, circulate this report) in your organization? Why or why not?"

- "What central themes about _____ can we pull out from this?"

- "From your perspective, what are the main points of view in this presentation?"

- "After hearing (experiencing, discussing) this, what do you think your chances of success are?"

- "Would you recommend this video to other groups? Why or why not?"

- "What other projects are you aware of that have objectives and issues similar to this one?"

  Probe: "What can you learn from those projects?"

- "How are people with special needs affected by this approach?"

More "So What?" Questions Focused on Meaning and Fit:

4

_____

_____

_____

_____

_____

Focus: Organizations and the nature of work

- "How does this report fit with what you already know about this issue in your organization?"

- "What does this presentation or document suggest to you about the current situation in your group or organization?"

- "What guiding principles or rules of thumb do you see operating here? Are they appropriate for your organization?"

- "What parts of this morning's discussion have potential positive impacts for your organization?"

- "Does this approach fit with how your organization does things?"

- "What are some differences between the reality presented in this video (report, presentation) and the reality in your organization? What are some similarities?"

- "How is this result significant for your organization?"

- "What values about workplaces are demonstrated in this video that you would like to either take on or avoid?"

- "What does all this suggest to you about best practices in this area?"

- "If you could offer some feedback to one of the consultants in this film to improve her interpersonal skills, what would you say and why?"

  Variation: Replace "improve her interpersonal skills" with other options.

- "What core organizational values would support what we have been discussing here today?"

- Worksheet during a presentation: "Following are the three key points this morning's speaker will be making. During this presentation, please rate your organization on each of these key elements."

- "On a scale of 1 to 5, where 1 is low and 5 is high, what relevance does all this have for your workplace?"

- "Does this video support your own experience? Please explain."

- "What potential consequences does this approach have for your organization?"

- "What does your organization want to get out of all this? What do you (as an individual) want to get out of all this?"

- "What issues in your organization are similar to those discussed by the speaker? What issues in your organization are different from those discussed by the speaker?"

- "Which result of this report has the most meaning for your organization? Why?"

- "How does this relate to your situation at work?"

- "When and how do you deal with issues on this topic in your organization?"

- "What aspects of this problem are non-negotiable in your area of the organization?"

- "What do you predict would happen in your department if you tried the approach suggested in this report?"

- "What are the consequences of doing nothing in your organization in relation to the conclusions of this meeting?"

- "What generalizations can you make about your organization in relation to the information in this presentation?"

- "Who benefits from the way things are now in your organization? How do they benefit? Who is disadvantaged by the way things are now? How are they disadvantaged?"

- "What did you find most useful about this presentation?"

- "What additional questions does this presentation raise for you as a senior manager in your organization?"

4

- What were your hopes and expectations when you first joined this group? To what extent have these been realized?

- "If you were building a scrapbook on this subject for your organization's archives, what memorable incidents or 'defining moments' would you include?"

More "So What?" Questions Focused on Organizations and the Nature of Work:

4

Focus: Personal development

- "What kinds of things mentioned in this report have you already tried in this area?"

    Probe: "How did they work out? What other things have you considered doing?"

- "What does this information suggest to you about yourself and those you work with?"

- "What values about leadership stood out for you in the film?"

    Probe: "Who saw something different here?"

- "How do these suggestions fit with your own projects in this area?"

- "What do you see as the complicating factors in this approach for someone in your position?"

- "Which of these guiding principles for organizations are also applicable to families?"

    Probe: "How are they applicable? Examples?"

- "Does this approach remind you of anything in your experience?"

- "What do these ideas get associated with in your mind?"

- "What are the implications of this discussion for your own immediate work environment?"

- "If this were your presentation, how might you have done it differently?"

- "What sort of 'real world', day-to-day problems or issues in your life come to mind when you reflect on this presentation?"

- "Does this learning experience have any significant meaning in your life?"

    Probe: "If yes, what does it mean?"

- "How does all this fit together for you?"

    Critical insight often occurs unexpectedly. The moments when people break through habitual ways of interpreting some idea, action, or social structure cannot be predicted in advance. It is not uncommon to be thinking about some aspect of one's life and experience a sudden flash of insight concerning an apparently unrelated area.[30]

More "So What?" Questions Focused on Personal Development:

4

"Now What?" – The Application Questions: Actions

WHAT?
THE NOTICE QUESTIONS

ACTIONS

OBSERVATIONS

NOW WHAT?
THE APPLICATION QUESTIONS

SO WHAT?
THE MEANING QUESTIONS

REFLECTIONS

Application questions lead to personal and organizational change by building owner-ship and through planning and implementation. The following "Now What?" questions are grouped into four main areas: personal change, organizational change, building ownership and operational planning and implementation.

Focus: Personal change

- "What is one thing you would like to do more of in your work situation? What is one thing you would like to do less of in your work situation?"

- "Now what? Let's look back at what you wanted when you completed the needs assessment for this session. Did you get what you wanted from this process? What are your next steps?"

- "Name three changes you could make in your family life that would reduce the amount of distress in your life today."

    Variation: Substitute "work unit" for "family life".

- "As a result of today's meeting, what is one thing you could start doing? Stop doing? Continue doing?"

    Suggestion: Use these three questions as the basis for a workshop journal.

- "What is one attitude you saw that you would like to have as a leader?"

    Probe: "How can you make that happen?"

- "Please note your top two areas for desired change on the page provided. Then put it in the envelope, seal it and address it to yourself. I will mail it to you in three months as a reminder of your commitment."

- "What is one thing you will do differently as a result of participating in this session?"

- "How could you behave more effectively as a result of your participation in this process? What is the first thing you will do to get started?"

- "What did you learn here that you would like to transfer into your situation back home? What support do you need to make that transference happen?"

    Tip: "Back home" may mean in your workplace or family situation. Be explicit.

- "Based on your experience and the conclusions in this report, what tips would you give to someone new in this area?"

- "What is one thing you learned here that applies to your life outside your workplace?"

    Probe: "What are the implications of this learning for personal change?"

4

More "Now What?" Questions Focused on Personal Change:

4

Focus: Organizational change

- "What is one simple step you could take when you go back to your office that would have a positive impact in this area for your organization?"

    Probe: "When will you take this step? How will others in this group know that you have done it? What will be the benefits of doing it?"

- "What is one thing you heard about here that you don't want to have in your organization?"

    Probe: "How can you prevent that happening?"

- "How relevant were our discussions to your day-to-day work situation?"

- "What was your original objective (organizational) for participating in this process? Have you met this objective?"

- "What conditions will you need to create in your organization so that you can successfully implement the changes you want to make?"

- "How else can you apply what you have learned in this experience to your organization?"

- "What will you have to do to make this work in your environment?"

- "How threatening will this change be to our employees? Why? How can we help prepare them for this change?"

More "Now What?" Questions Focused on Organizational Change:

_____

_____

_____

_____

Focus: Building ownership

- "Who is already on board with this approach? Who is partly on board? Who is not on board at all?"

  Probe: "How do we ensure we have the people we need on board? What action can we take to get them on board?"

- "Who may be excluded as a result of this new approach? What can you do (if anything) to accommodate these people?"

- "Whom should we acknowledge or thank for their contributions and involvement to date?"

- "At what point in this process should we consult with others who are less directly involved but who have an impact on how we implement this?"

- "How can we transfer ownership for the plan from this small group to the entire organization?"

- "What approaches can we take that will motivate people to collaborate with us on the next steps?"

- "How can we build mindshare for our account plan with other areas in our organization?"

- "Are there any existing or potential personality conflicts in our organization that could get in the way of us achieving our goals?"

  Probe: "How can we address these now to prevent problems later on?"

- "How are you going to build ownership for making some changes in your department in relation to what you have learned here?"

4

- "When you begin to implement these changes in your organization, where do you expect the trouble spots to be? Why? What can you do to ensure you are prepared to address potential problems?"

More "Now What?" Questions Focused on Building Ownership:

4

Focus: Operational planning and implementation

- "If you could get any one key person you wanted to participate in helping with the implementation of this project, whom would you pick? Why?"

    Probe: "If that person isn't appropriate (for any reason) is there someone else or a combination of other people who could provide the same insights, energy and experience?"

- "What driving or supportive forces will enable you to implement this plan? What restraining or inhibiting forces could put blocks in your way?"

- "Do you need approval from anyone to proceed with implementing your plan?"

- "What specialized skills or knowledge do you require to be successful in implementing this plan?"

- "What kind of human and financial resources do we need to support this work?"

- "Who will be responsible for communication related to this plan?"

- "Who will be responsible for monitoring and evaluating success in relation to the changes being made?"

- "What kinds of power will it take to act on this plan in our organization?"

- "What have we learned about implementing plans in previous situations in our organization? How can we use this information to help pave the way for this plan?"

- "What are some dos and don'ts that you are going to follow in your organization when applying what you have learned here?"

- "Based on what you have learned here, what could you do personally to ensure that the changes you are making will go as smoothly as possible?"

- "What lessons have you learned elsewhere that will be useful now that we are about to take action on this project?"

- "How realistic is this plan given available resources?"

4

87

- "In a year's time, how will we know whether we have been successful?"

- "What is one thing that each of us can do to support the implementation of this approach?"

- "Now that we have made this decision, what are the implications for our team (organization) over the next three months? Six months? A year? Two years?"

- "How reasonable are our timelines for implementation?"

- "What is our Achilles heel on this project?"

- "What potential is there in this plan for increasing conflict among key stakeholders? What potential is there in this plan for decreasing conflict among key stakeholders?"

    Probe: "How do we want to accommodate the potential for conflict as we implement this plan?"

- "Whose influence do we need to get this done?"

- "Think about the structure of our organization. How will that structure support what we want to do? Hamper what we want to do?"

- "What are the key outcomes that we want? What are our secondary outcomes?"

- "What skills and experience do we have in this group that will support the implementation of this plan? What additional skills and experience will we need to be successful?"

More "Now What?" Questions Focused on Operational Planning and Implementation:

Recommended Reading

Argyris, Chris, Robert Putnam and Diana McLain Smith. *Action Science.* San Francisco, CA: Jossey-Bass, 1985.

Dotlich, David and Peter Cairo. *Action Coaching.* San Francisco, CA: Jossey-Bass, 1999.

Gaw, Beverly. "Processing Questions: an Aid to Completing the Learning Cycle." In *The 1979 Annual Handbook for Group Facilitators.* La Jolla, CA: University Associates, 1979.

Heron, John. *Group Facilitation: Theories and Models for Practice.* London, UK: Kogan Page, 1993.

Introduction to "Structured Experiences." In *The 1980 Annual Handbook for Group Facilitators.* La Jolla, CA: University Associates, 1980.

Reinharz, Shulamit. "Implementing New Paradigm Research: a Model for Training and Practice." Chapter 36 of *Human Inquiry*, edited by Peter Reason and John Rowan. Toronto, ON: John Wiley and Sons, 1981.

4

Chapter 5

Questions for Thinking Critically

Effective questioning is an essential component of critical thinking – an examination of how and why things are done the way they are. Critical thinking leads towards deeper understanding and is based on open mindedness, active inquiry and increased awareness and sensitivity.

Critical thinking is an essential skill in situations involving complex problem solving. It doesn't necessarily move towards action *per se,* but it does move towards a clearer understanding of a situation, which is an essential prerequisite for determining effective action. Facilitators encourage critical thinking in a variety of situations, such as the following:

- There is a need to hear a variety of views on an issue, to develop optional strategies or to explore more than one way of doing things.

- Participants are challenging why things are done the way they are.

- You want to raise awareness among participants that how things are done is closely related to a specific context and period in time.

- Participants could be more sensitive to the situations of others or more alert to their own feelings and those of others, especially in situations involving an imbalance of power.

Critical thinking stimulates group members to learn together. It encourages participants to explore their experiences, ideas, assumptions and beliefs about a topic as a way to discover their own "truth" in relation to that topic.

Come on now, we're going to go build a mirror factory first and put out nothing but mirrors for the next year and take a long look in them.[31]

Commitment to the truth does not mean seeking the Truth – the absolute final word or ultimate cause. Rather, it means a relentless willingness to root out the ways we limit or deceive ourselves from seeing what is, and to continually challenge our theories of why things are the way they are. It means continually broadening our awareness, just as the great athlete with extraordinary peripheral vision keeps trying to "see more of the playing field".[32]

The first step in moving towards critical thinking is to ask thoughtful questions.

> *Reflective skepticism is not outright cynicism, nor is it contemptuous dismissal of all things new. It is, rather, the belief that claims for the universal validity and applicability of an idea or practice must be subject to a careful testing against each individual's experiences. It is being wary of uncritically accepting an innovation, change, or new perspective simply because it is new. It is not to be equated with resistance to change.*[33]

The Art Gallery of Ontario (Canada) uses critically reflective questions to encourage patrons to consider works of art in a variety of dimensions. The following questions appeared in an exhibit (March, 2001) on naked bodies.

> *Who decides what beauty is? Are naked bodies always erotic? Who says what it is to be feminine or masculine?*

> (near paintings and sculptures by masters such as Jules Pacquin, Kees van Dongen, Auguste Rodin, Alberto Giacommetti)

> *Do women have to be naked to get into the Metropolitan Museum of Art? Less than 5% of the artists in the Modern Art sections are women, but 85% of the nudes are female.*

> (on the 1989 poster "Guerilla Girrls" of a reclining female nude with a guerilla head)

Questions to support critical thinking are included in this chapter for four areas:

1. making assumptions and perspectives explicit

2. understanding interests and power relationships

3. exploring alternative ways of thinking and acting

4. doing the right thing.

For each area, three perspectives are provided: the individual, the organization and the broader context.

> *With regard to these questions and activities, there are no right answers (though there might be many wrong answers). The questions are not meant to be tests. Their value should be in the self-searching they inspire and the discussions they provoke.*[34]

5

Guidelines for Questions on Thinking Critically

The following guidelines support facilitators in developing a climate for critical thinking. Use the blank space at the right-hand side of the page to check off the guidelines that you would like to emphasize more.

a. Develop a comfortable climate for participants in which candour and critical reflection are important norms for working together. A supportive atmosphere gives people permission to think critically. _____

b. Support participants who ask difficult or awkward reflective questions by commenting positively when they do so. For example, "Nice question" or "These are important questions – they may make us feel uncomfortable but that's probably a sign that we should be thinking about this" or "Let's explore this tension a little further – this usually leads to constructive discussions." _____

c. Model critical reflection by being open to new perspectives, by challenging assumptions and by welcoming diversity and different ways of thinking. _____

d. Initiate critical thinking using both positive and negative events and situations. If you only use negative situations, participants may come to think that critical thinking is a negatively based function. For example, "Yesterday's meeting was efficient, fun and very productive. What were we doing that made us so successful?" _____

e. Explore the assumptions underlying various perspectives of group members: "When you state your position that way, what assumptions are you making?" _____

f. Enable participants to disclose and discuss differences between the way things are supposed to work and the way things actually work: "This video presents an ideal situation for implementing organizational change. How does it look in comparison to the day-to-day reality of life in your organization?" _____

5

g.	Provide participants with opportunities to reflect on what they are discussing through time for talking with others, reading articles and so on.	_____

h.	Move from specific to general. Participants are usually more comfortable with critical thinking if you begin a question or a discussion with a specific situation and then work towards broader implications. For example, hold up a recent newspaper article about a protest that is linked in some way or another to the group and ask, "What would you protest about publicly in relation to the issue we are discussing?"	_____

i.	Critical thinking involves getting underneath the surface. Ask questions that clarify or expose whose interests are being served in a particular situation. Explore who stands to benefit or lose as a result of changes you may be considering.	_____

j.	Act ethically. As facilitators, we are bound by an ethical imperative to point out to group members, learners and clients the potential risks involved in various change efforts that might result from intensive critical scrutiny of a situation. Check your workshop design with your client or supervisor to ensure that she is comfortable with the risks involved in exploring questions that have a critical thinking element.	_____

k.	Critical thinking takes time. Ideas need to ferment; people need to test how ideas feel, exploring their assumptions and values. Ensure that you have adequate time in your agenda for critical thinking.	_____

l.	Know when to stop thinking and move towards action. Critical thinking can go on and on and take you to some very interesting places that lead nowhere.	_____

5

Making Assumptions and Perspectives Explicit

I have often found that differences of opinion result from different sets of assumptions. To deal with these differences, one needs to examine the validity of the assumptions behind them.
(An executive-facilitator)

Critical thinking enables participants to be aware of what other group members are thinking, what the assumptions are about a topic being discussed and how their perspectives and those of others fit or don't fit.

The following questions help to make assumptions and perspectives more explicit in group settings.

Focus: The individual

- "What comes to mind when you hear the phrase 'corporate loyalty'?"

    Variation: Substitute other phrases to surface individual perspectives in other areas.

- "What kinds of behaviours make you feel good about a supervisor? What kinds of behaviours make you feel uneasy or uncomfortable about a supervisor?"

    Suggestion: Develop the list of responses into a checklist on healthy behaviours for supervisors.

- "What are the implications of your 'personal style' in terms of your role as a member of this task force (organization, corporation, group)?"

- "What kinds of activities in your day-to-day work make you feel good (or not good) about your current position?"

    Probe: "Why do you feel good (or not good) about these activities? What could you do to feel better on a consistent basis about the work you do?"

- "What is your bottom line on . . . . . ?"

- "What helped to shape your opinions about . . . . . ?"

- "What is an unspoken assumption that you have about the outcome of this meeting?"

More Questions Focused on the Individual:

5

Focus: The organization

- "What assumptions about organizations are at the heart of this approach (issue, decision)? Do you agree with these assumptions? Explain."

- "What are the all possible positions a person in your organization could take on this issue?"

- "What do you think the president of this company needs to hear from employees to make sound decisions about the future directions of the organization? Summarize your input in a single sentence."

- "The slogan 'Think globally, act locally' (or some other slogan) is widely used today. Does this slogan have any relevance for your organization? Why or why not?"

    Probe: "What are some examples?"

- "How often do you speak out on topics or issues related to your organization's mission and values?"

    Probe: "Do you speak out with your own immediate team? With others in your professional community? In your larger community?"

- "Imagine that you have been asked as an external consultant to evaluate the performance of members of a Board of Directors over the past two years. What aspects of board performance would you consider? Why?"

- "What criteria should we use to determine who is involved in a task force on this issue?"

- "Individual experiences in organizations often reflect broader organizational issues that need to be addressed. What experiences have you had as a manager in this organization that point to broader organizational issues that need to be addressed?"

- "What two key events (critical incidents) stand out in your mind as defining (or being typical of) how your organization functions? Please explain."

- "What is one aspect of your work environment that has a toxic and stressful impact on you? If you were in charge, what would you do to reduce the toxicity and distress?"

    Probe: "How do you think things worked out this way?"

- "What is going on now in your organization that causes you to feel optimistic about the future? What is going on now in your organization that causes you to feel pessimistic about the future?"

    There's nothing more debauched than thinking.
    This sort of wantonness runs wild like a wind-borne weed on a
    plot laid out for daisies.

    Nothing's sacred for those who think.
    Calling things brazenly by name,
    risqué analyses, salacious syntheses,
    frenzied, rakish chases after the bare facts,
    the filthy fingering of touchy subjects,
    discussion in heat - it's music to their ears.

    Wislawa Szymborska[35]

- "What's your best hunch about what this organization will look like in three years' time if it continues on its current path and strategies?"

- "From your perspective, what are the main characteristics of our organization's culture?"

    Probe: "Which of these characteristics are you comfortable with? Uncomfortable with?"

5

- "When you think about the future of this company (group, organization), would you describe yourself as leaning more towards optimism or towards pessimism? Why?"

More Questions Focused on the Organization:

5

Focus: The broader context

- "What are the popular perceptions about this issue in our country?"

    Probe: "Do you agree with these perceptions? Why or why not? Whom do you know who shares these perceptions?"

- "What are the first words or phrases that come to mind when you hear the word 'poverty'? How do these initial words and phrases reflect your perception of this issue in our country?"

    Variation: Substitute other words and phrases for the word "poverty": "crime", "older people", "wealth", "incompetence", "best practices".

- Provide participants with an article that includes statistics on an issue you are discussing and then select questions such as the following to stimulate a discussion about perspectives:
  - "What do these statistics mean to you?"
  - "How might these statistics be interpreted by the president of your corporation?"
  - "How might these statistics be interpreted by a minister in a fundamentalist church?"
  - "How might these statistics be interpreted by a politician in the middle of a re-election campaign?"
  - "How might these statistics be interpreted by the head of your local advocacy group on this issue?"
  - "How might these statistics be interpreted by a reporter for a tabloid newspaper?"
  - "Does this perspective we are discussing provide a model of the world (as you see things now) or for the world (as you would like things to be)?"[36]

5

- "Consider the following quotation:

  Asking awkward questions about the rightness of, and justification for, political decisions, actions, and structures is the focus of critical thinking about the political world.[37]

  What 'awkward questions' need to be asked about racism in our country?"

  Variation: Substitute other words and phrases for the word "racism": "health care", "infrastructure support", "youth offenders", "access for people with disabilities", "misuse", "social support funds".

- "What themes do you see frequently in the popular media about this issue? To what extent do you agree with these themes?"

- "What factors in our current environment are supportive of how we work together now? What factors in our current environment are challenging how we work together?"

- Choose a newspaper, magazine, journal article, audiotape or radio interview with a clear point of view and ask participants to consider the following questions:
  - "What are your overall impressions?"
  - "Do the opinions in the article reflect one or more points of view?"
  - "How is information used in the article? Does it support a particular point of view?"
  - "Does the language or terminology indicate any particular bias?"
  - "Who benefits from the views expressed?"
  - "Who bears the costs of the views expressed?"
  - "Are these views supportive of or contrary to your own point of view?"
  - "How legitimate is the information source?"
  - "How are statistics used in the article? Are the statistics valid and relevant?"
  - "Does the information presented support the main points of the article?"
  - "Do you know of any important information that is not presented in the article?"[38]

- "What metaphors do you hear or see in the media in relation to this issue (e.g., couch potatoes, heartless industrialists, bleeding heart liberals)?"

- "In what ways do the issues in your organization reflect current trends and concerns in society in general?"

More Questions Focused on the Broader Context:

Understanding Interests and Power Relationships

In sociopolitical terms, thinking critically entails the habit and ability of asking awkward questions. Questions such as "Why are nearly all faculty at my college white, and nearly all the service staff black or Hispanic?" Questions such as "How can a government condemn other countries' shipments of arms to a nation as wrong, when we're doing the same thing secretly?"

. . . Being critically alert also means being able to make connections between personal circumstances (such as the closing of a local health facility, a farm foreclosure or the appearance of more street people in a town) and broader political happenings (cutting health services budgets, removing farm subsidies, or adopting community mental health policies and consequently reducing residential care for the mentally ill).[39]

The following questions enable group members to explore and understand whose interests are at the heart of a discussion and how power influences perspectives, decision making and outcomes. Given the nature of these questions, pay particular attention to your delivery style (body language, tone of voice and inflection) so that your inquiries aren't perceived to be biased.

Focus: The individual

- "Whose interests are being served in this situation?"

    Probe: "How is this happening?"

- "Whose interests are <u>not</u> being served in this situation?"

    Probe: "How is this happening?"

- "Think about the leaders in this organization (sector) who have the most influence and positional power. Whom do you identify with the most? Why?"

- Who will experience a change in profile as a result of participating in or supporting this project?

  Probe: "Describe the expected change and its impact on these individuals."

- "Who stands to benefit from leaving things the way they are? Who stands to lose?"

- "Who stands to benefit from the changes we are considering? Who stands to lose?"

More Questions Focused on the Individual:

5

Focus: The organization

- "What key incidents in our history have helped shape the way we are organized?"

- "Complete the following two sentences: Formally and on paper, real power in our organization lies with … Informally and in practice, real power in our organization lies with …"

- "What do people argue about most in our organization?"

  Probe: "What is at stake in these arguments?"

- "Who has the greatest potential for gain as a result of this crisis (decision, change process)? Who has the greatest potential for loss as a result of this crisis (decision, change process)?"

- "To what degree (a lot? a little?) is information used as power in our organization?"

  Probe: "How is information shared?"

> *Questions are the best tool you have to help people explore what they don't know.*[40]

- "What kinds of information do you consider as private in your organization, that is, not to be known outside of the organization?"

  Probe: "Why should this information be kept private?"

- "What are the first words that come to mind to describe how this group functions?"

  Probe: "What made you choose those words? Give specific incidents as examples."

- "When you hear the phrase 'positive use of power', who comes to mind in your organization?"

  Probe: Ask for specific examples.

- "What is the dominant colour that comes to mind when you think about how your group (organization) functions? Why did you choose this colour?"

  Probe: "What would you like the dominant colour to be? Please explain."

  Variations: Substitute other words and phrases for the word "colour": "sound", "car", "animal".

- "You are being interviewed 'off the record and confidentially' by a reporter from a prestigious business magazine who asks, 'Who is really in charge in your organization?' What do you reply?"

- "What is one aspect of how we are structured that works well for us? What can we do to ensure that it continues to work well?"

  Variation: "What is one aspect of how we are structured that doesn't work well for us? What can we do to improve this aspect?"

- "Complete the following sentences:

  - If we had _____ involved in this issue then we could make the changes we think are essential.

  - In our organization we make decisions as if _____ . We would function better if we made decisions as if _____ "

  Probe: "How can we make our "ifs" a reality?"

More Questions Focused on the Organization:

_____

_____

_____

_____

_____

Focus: The broader context

- "How are decisions made (e.g., consensus, voting, authority) about major issues in our community?"

    Probes: "Is there a difference between how high-risk decisions are made and how other types of decisions are made? Are people comfortable with how decisions are made?"

- "People often find it difficult to ask for things that they think are important in society. When you think about the issue of _____ in our country today, what would you like to ask your government for? What are the risks involved in making this request?"

    Probe: "How could you get others involved in making this request?"

- "What are the potential benefits of being a strong leader in this sector? What are the potential costs?"

- "Consider and respond to the following quotation in light of the _____ strike in our province:

    The late Everett Hughes, a pioneering sociologist of the professions, once observed that the professions have struck a bargain with society. In return for access to their extraordinary knowledge in matters of great human importance, society has granted them a mandate for social control in their fields of specialization, a high degree of autonomy in their practice, and a license to determine who shall assume the mantle of professional authority (Hughes, 1959). But in the current climate of criticism, controversy, and dissatisfaction, the bargain is coming unstuck. When the professions' claim to extraordinary knowledge is so much in question, why should we continue to grant them extraordinary rights and privileges.[41]

    Variation: Use other quotations to prompt critical reflection with group members.

- "With what other organizations are we interdependent?"

  Probes: "How are we interdependent?" "What is the impact of this interdependence on us?" "What is the impact of this interdependence on our publics?" "Who benefits most from this interdependence?" "Who suffers as a result of this interdependence?"

- "What hard choices do we need to make in relation to community priorities and resources?"

  Probe: "What values should guide how we make these choices?"

- ""Do we ever inadvertently create problems for those with whom we are interdependent?"

  Probes: "How does this happen?" "Why does this happen?" "What is the impact of this interdependence on our publics/customers?" "How can we prevent this happening in the future?" "If this happens in the future, how can we respond in support of our interdependency?"

More Questions Focused on the Broader Context:

5

Exploring Alternative Ways of Thinking and Acting

Facilitators need questions that stimulate participants to be creative when discussing challenges and problems. The following questions encourage people to look at new ways of approaching old situations – to explore innovative approaches to challenges and dilemmas.

Focus: The individual

- "Think of someone whom you consider to be a leader in your organization in the area we are discussing. What do you think her position would be on this issue as it affects your organization?"

    Probe: "What is your position on this issue?"

- "Think of someone in your organization who is skilled at critical thinking. In preparation for our next session, discuss this topic with that person and ask for his insights."

- "If you were the president of this company, what would be your first course of action to address this situation?"

- "Think about an important goal that you have achieved in your life. What factors (e.g., personal characteristics, support systems, attitudes) helped you to achieve that goal? To what extent could those factors be helpful to you in this situation?"

- "Describe the ideal workplace for you or someone in your position. Describe this workplace in terms of physical space, location, hours, colleagues, remuneration, benefits and stress."

- "Imagine that it is three years from today and this issue has been completely resolved to your satisfaction. What is going on that is different from today?"

- "What is one thing that needs to happen to make you feel better about your workplace (board of directors' meetings, personal productivity)?"

- "Think of a political decision that has had a significant impact on your life (e.g., closing a school, a major change in the health care system, a decision to have mandatory military service). Describe the impact on your life. Describe the benefits that your government expected from this decision. What was the final result from your perspective in terms of a cost–benefit analysis?"

- "What is the first thing you would do if tomorrow you became the chairperson of your organization's board of directors? How could you achieve the same result over the next few months without becoming chairperson?"

- A preferred scenario is a detailed, concrete description of a desired state. People are helped to construct preferred scenarios by asking and answering a series of questions such as the following:

  - "What would this problem look like if it were managed better?"

  - "What changes would take place in my present lifestyle?"

  - "What would I be doing differently with the people in my life?"

  - "What patterns of behaviour would be in place that currently are not?"

  - "What patterns of behaviour that are currently in place would be eliminated?"

  - "What would exist that does not exist now?"

  - "What would be happening that does not happen now?"

  - "What would I have that I do not have now?"

  - "What decisions would be made and executed?"

  - "What accomplishments would be in place that are not now?[42]

- "Imagine that it is two years from today and I am a reporter from a high-profile magazine in your sector. I have heard about how you have turned around a difficult situation and have come to interview you so that others in your situation can benefit from learning about what you have done. Think back to two years ago. What were the biggest problems you were facing? What did you decide to do? What risks were involved in your decision? What is different now from two years ago?"

  Probe: Ask for differences in both work and personal life.

- "If a 10-year-old were asked to address this issue, what would he do?"

- "What are our best intentions with respect to addressing this issue?"

- "What might be a left-leaning political leader's take on this situation? What might be a right-leaning political leader's take on this situation?"

- "If you could have three great thinkers or leaders in your field on this task force, who would they be? What do you think they would suggest as options for action in this situation?"

- "It is two years from today and you have followed your gut instinct to take a big chance on this project. As a result of your risky initiative things are going really well. What did you do to create this positive future? What risks were involved? How did you address these risks?"

More Questions Focused on the Individual:

Focus: The organization

- "How does this approach fit with your organization's culture?"

- "What do you feel good about with respect to how your organization has responded to the current situation? What do you feel disappointed about with respect to how your organization has responded to the current situation?"

- "How have we done this in the past? What did we learn that could help us now?"

- "Think about the current situation we are discussing. What are all the possible answers that you think organizational change experts might recommend?"

    Probe: "Consultants sometimes create a 'hammer' and then see lots of situations as potential 'nails'. Which of these answers could be potential nails and which could be real solutions for your particular situation?"

- "Let's check this draft list of strategic priorities against our company mission. Do they fit well or do we need to make some adjustments?"

- "What are the risks (potential harmful consequences) for our organization in each of the suggested alternatives?"

- "What are our options for when we should act on this situation? Given the benefits and risks involved, what is the best time to act?"

- "Have our organizational values shifted at all over the past five years? If yes, how and why? If no, why not?"

- "Draw a horizontal line on your page. At the far right end write 'most expensive' and at the far left end write 'least expensive'. In the next five minutes, work with a partner to generate all the alternatives you can think of that would fit on this continuum."

    Probe: Ask them to complete continua for different extremes, for example, most risky, least risky.

- "What are the potential consequences for your organization of doing nothing about the current situation? What are the potential consequences of making a decision to …?"

- "Whom could you count on to support you if you made some significant changes in how this group functions?"

More Questions Focused on the Organization:

Focus: The broader context

- "Where else have you seen this approach work?"

    Probe: "What are the key features that make it work in that setting?"

- "What other groups (companies, organizations, countries) have been faced with this situation? What did they do? "

    Probes: "How was their context similar to or different from ours? What happened as a result of their actions? What implications does their experience have for us?"

- "How do other cultures approach this issue?"

- "Consider the following quotation:

    The right of the individual is the power that upholds the right of the community, just as, conversely, it is the community that upholds and defends the rights of the individual.[43]

    In what ways do we as individuals support our community? How do we as a community support the rights of individuals in our community?"

- "Think of a situation in your province or state where the division between the haves and the have-nots is significant in relation to the issue being discussed.

    - Why does this situation exist?

    - What perspectives are there on what to do about the situation?

    - Develop a list of conditions (outcomes) to describe a successful solution to this situation.

    - Brainstorm all the possible solutions you can think of.

    - Play your optional solutions against the list of conditions and choose a possible approach.

    - Consider the risks and benefits of your chosen approach before confirming that it is a wise choice."

More Questions Focused on the Broader Context:

5

Doing the Right Thing

Doing the right thing depends on being clear about your values and how you act on them, that is, your ethical standards. Similarly, organizations function better when the people involved are clear about what their values are and how they act on them.

> *Today it's not just a matter of deciding right from wrong. Often as not, we have to decide between right and right, and wrong and wrong. In our times, as Camus said, we are clear that the cry for clean hands that might come from making exactly "right" decisions is the cry of a damned soul. There are no clean hands. For many people who appreciate their own degree of moral probity this is painful. The fact is that our time uses a different metaphor and a different set of principles. In many situations we have to deal with, there are no rules. We have only our critical intelligence to determine what is really needed. Today, we ask not what is right, but what is responsible. Not what is good or bad, but what is befitting or appropriate. Not whether it is honest or pure, but whether it is necessary and responsible.*[44]

> *The values of the individual employee are intrinsic to the achievement of our business objectives.*
> *(A manager-facilitator)*

Facilitators can encourage participants to think about ethics in many situations: to understand points of view, to explore ethical dilemmas, to raise awareness about potential wrong doing, to consider the impact of decisions on other stakeholders or to explore issues related to power. The following questions encourage participants to consider how to do the right thing – that is, the ethics of situations.

Focus: The individual

- "What are the values that underlie this point of view?"

- "Think about yourself when you were a new employee coming into this company. How did you want to be treated?"

    Probe: "Is this how you treat the people you supervise now?"

- "Do you agree or disagree with the statement, 'How we work in our organization reflects the personal philosophy of our president'? Please explain, using specific examples."

    The golden rule: do unto others as you would like them to do unto you.

- "What kinds of ethical dilemmas does this initiative present for you?"

    The toughest ethical issues have no right or wrong, no black or white, but shades of grey. Every choice has costs. This is the definition of an ethical dilemma. Not only is there no right or wrong, but coaches in good conscience differ about which is the lesser evil.[45]

- "What is one thing you learned as a child that has helped shape your political orientation?"

- "Imagine that it is New Year's Eve and you are sitting down with the president and vice-president of your board of directors to make resolutions for the year to come. What is one value you would encourage these two leaders to act on over the coming year?"

- "What would push you to make a radical change in your lifestyle? Think of something significant, for example, that affects how you support yourself, or with whom you spend time, or how you act on your beliefs."

- "Assume that you have been recruited to a new job with a firm that does corporate takeovers. This firm is thinking of taking over your previous employer (i.e., your current employer) and they ask you for advice on what the new president should do to increase bottom line profits and improve employee morale. What would you advise the new president to do?"

- "Who are the most important people in your life? What do these people contribute to your life? How do you contribute to their lives?"

- "How is the current situation consistent (or inconsistent) with your values?"

- "Think of an incident that makes you feel good about your organization. What is it about this incident that makes you feel good?"

  Probe: "What is the value that is at play in this incident?"

- "Think about someone you admire in your organization (group). What do you admire about how that person acts? What is the value that underlies such behaviour?"

  Probe: "How do you act on that value in your life? What could you do more of (or less of) to enhance how you implement that value in your life?"

- "What is one rule that you grew up with that you think is important for raising children today? What is one rule that you grew up with that you would not use with your children today?"

- "How did your parents express their expectations about ethical behaviour to you? Give an example of an expectation."

More Questions Focused on the Individual:

5

Focus: The organization

- "What are the three most important values you hold as a board member for this health charity?"

   Probe: "From your perspective, how operational are these values in how this organization conducts business?"

- "Describe a critical incident that occurred within the last six months and that demonstrates how senior managers act on organizational values. Name the value in question."

   Suggestion: Ask participants to choose an incident that stands out for them; it may be either positive or negative in relation to organizational values.

> *When business logic asks, Where is the advantage? Ethical logic asks, How does this decision affect the dignity of others? Over time, this question evolves into a combined and interactive one: What business advantage serves dignity? And how can the advancing of human dignity toward customers, employees, partners, suppliers and the community add to competitive advantage?[46]*

5

- "Think about how this group works together. In what areas are you comfortable being candid with one another? In what areas are you less comfortable being candid with one another?"

   Probe: "How could you expand the degree of candour in the group?"

- "What values does your organization espouse (either formally through a strategic plan, or informally through leadership)?"

   Probe: "If you could change one thing that would make your organization more ethical, what would it be?

- "How do our board of directors and chief executive officer signal their ethical expectations?"[47]

  Probe: "How is senior management accountable for ethical performance? How are shareholders engaged in issues and decisions regarding ethical performance?"

- "What criteria should guide how we make decisions during this process?"

  Probe: "How will we know that we have made the right decisions?"

- "Who will this decision affect? How will it affect them? How comfortable would you be if you had to live with the impact of this decision?"

- "Whom are you responsible for (obligated to) when you make this decision? How are you reflecting this responsibility in how you make this decision?"

- "What is your organization's greatest achievement? How do you contribute to that achievement?"

- "What two or three words would you like people to associate with your organization?"

- "You have been assigned as mentor to a new employee (board member, group member) who will be taking your place when you move to a new position. This person has asked you what he should do to build positive working relationships with subordinates. What would you tell this person?"

- "How do you encourage the national office employees in your labour union to engage in critical thinking for the benefit of members?"

- "Think of your organization as a growing person. How mature is it? Is it a newborn, a young child, an adolescent, a young adult, a mature adult or an older person? Explain your response with specific examples."

- "How does this organization express its expectations about ethical behaviour to employees and board members? Give an example of an expectation."

5

- "How fair are our charity's practices with respect to donors, employees, stakeholders and the public?"

- "How does our organization support the health of employees through its human resource policies?"

More Questions Focused on the Organization:

Focus: The broader context

- "How does our organization participate in global ethical (or social justice) issues related to our industry?"

- "What do you think are the top two most important values for parents to teach their children in our society?"

    Probe: "To what extent are these values operational in your current life or work situation?"

- "What is our organization's reputation when it comes to ethical issues or 'doing the right thing'?"

- "How does our organization support the health of the community in which we are located?"

- "What injustices are you aware of in your community that you would like to see addressed?"

    Probes: "How could your organization play a useful role in addressing these injustices? Who in your organization could take the lead in this area?"

More Questions Focused on the Broader Context:

5

Recommended Reading

Brookfield, Stephen D. *Developing Critical Thinkers*. San Francisco, CA: Jossey-Bass, 1987.

Freire, Paulo. *Education for Critical Consciousness.* New York, NY: Seabury Press, 1973.

Laborde, Genie. *Influencing with Integrity.* Palo Alto, CA: Syntony Publishing, 1984.

Mezirow, Jack. *Fostering Critical Reflection in Adulthood.* San Francisco, CA: Jossey-Bass, 1991.

Postman, Neil, and Charles Weingartner. *Teaching as a Subversive Activity.* New York, NY: Delacorte Press, 1969.

Scholtes, Peter R. *The Leader's Handbook.* Toronto, ON: McGraw-Hill, 1998.

Stanfield, Brian R. *The Courage to Lead.* Transform Self, Transform Society. Toronto, ON: The Canadian Institute of Cultural Affairs (ICA Canada), 2000.

5

Chapter 6

Questions for Addressing Issues

Understanding and addressing issues is often a central part of facilitated processes, for example, in strategic planning, team development, network building, advocacy and general problem solving.

Focused and systematic questioning enables groups to have the meaningful conversations required to address issues competently. This chapter explores six main areas of inquiry when addressing issues through group processes:

1. identifying the issues
2. understanding the issues
3. generating options for action
4. testing options for action
5. making a decision
6. taking action.

Although these six steps appear here in a suggested chronological order, how you use the steps and related questions depends on the situation. We will often identify the issues and then develop a challenge statement for each one. Then the next steps follow as listed above. In some situations, steps 1, 2, 3 may have been completed by the client and the purpose of the process is to do steps 4, 5, 6.

It is essential to customize the process and the questions to suit your situation.

In the non-governmental sector in particular, many agencies are very well organized with respect to issues management, as the following excerpt from the Kidney Foundation of Canada's Advocacy Handbook illustrates.

> *Successful advocacy requires a proactive and systematic approach to issues management, usually over an extended period of time. The first four steps should be part of the ongoing activities of an advocacy group. The last three steps will be most important when the need to take action has been identified and agreed upon.*
>
> a. *Gathering intelligence: What's going on out there?*
> b. *Building relationships: Who should we be talking to?*
> c. *Identifying and analysing the issues: Whose problem is it anyway?*
> d. *Researching the issues: What else do we need to know?*
> e. *Developing a position: What are we going to say?*
> f. *Developing and implementing a strategy: What are we going to do?*
> g. *Evaluating the outcome: Are we there yet?*[48]

6

Guidelines for Addressing Issues

Questions for addressing issues usually fit within the context of a larger process. For example, in strategic planning they may guide the development of goals; in team development they may help to identify and understand team building challenges.

Use the blank space at the right-hand side of the page to check off the guidelines that you want to emphasize when addressing issues.

a. Confirm that your role as facilitator is to be content neutral and a process advocate. Be clear about the implications of this stance, i.e., your focus is on avoiding conflict of interest and ensuring a high quality decision making process, not influencing outcomes. (See *Chapter 2, Core Facilitation Values.*)   _____

b. Addressing issues requires a comprehensive approach to the context of an issue. For facilitators, this means that background information for discussing issues must be inclusive and representative of a variety of perspectives and orientations. Inclusiveness up front encourages ownership for solutions developed later on.   _____

c. Ensure that solutions take into account potential impacts on the whole system rather than on only one part of it.[49]   _____

d. Explore the terrain. Encourage participants to consider a variety of perspectives on an issue: "Does everyone have the same understanding of this situation? What other perspectives are in this group?"   _____

e. Encourage participants to go to where the tension is in a particular topic or during a discussion: "I'm getting the feeling that a particularly sensitive topic is at the heart of this issue." If participants agree, ask, "Where does all the tension come from?"   _____

f. Avoid questions that are actually indirect statements about issues: "How did such a negative spin get put on this problem?"   _____

6

g. If a discussion about issues is getting too abstract and conceptual, ask specific questions that focus participants on particular aspects or action steps that are practical in nature.   _____

h. Use lateral thinking techniques and processes (e.g., brainstorming, mind-mapping, open space technology) to encourage divergent thinking about issues and their solutions.   _____

1. *Creative thinkers reject standardized formats for problem solving.*
2. *They have interests in a wide range of related and divergent fields.*
3. *They can take multiple perspectives on a problem.*
4. *They view the world as relative and contextual rather than universal and absolute.*
5. *They frequently use trial-and-error methods in their experimentation with alternative approaches.*
6. *They have a future orientation; change is embraced optimistically as a valuable developmental possibility.*
7. *They have self-confidence and trust in their own judgment.*[50]

6

Identifying the Issues

- "Where are we most successful and productive as an organization? Where are we least successful and productive as an organization?"

- "What are the major external threats facing our organization over the next six months? How prepared are we to address these threats?"

- "What is going well in our community with respect to patient access to effective treatment? What do we need to improve with respect to patient access to effective treatment?"

- "What do we know about how well our society accommodates the needs of its elderly citizens?"

- "What are the underlying issues in our organization that affect how well we work together?"

- "How do we compare in terms of _____ to other organizations similar in purpose and size to us?"

- "Who are your biggest critics? What are they saying? What can you learn from this?"

- "What are our organization's strongest points when it comes to customer satisfaction? What are our organization's weakest points when it comes to customer satisfaction?"

> *I like to use these questions with my own company but they only work well if I don't get defensive, and sometimes that's pretty hard. I'm getting better at it. (A manager-facilitator)*

6

- "Think about how we do business in relation to this account. What are we good at? Where could we be better?"

- "Given our resources, what is one thing we could do to improve how we work together?"

- "Where do we agree as a management team on strategic directions? Where do we disagree?"

- "If you were in charge, what would be your top two priorities for change over the next two years to ensure a positive future for our organization?"

- "What do our press clippings say about us?"

- "What is one thing you think your deputy minister/chief executive officer/director/president should know about the current situation?"

- "From your perspective, what signs and symptoms indicate problems that need addressing?"

- "In what areas of our business do our staff have a low level of commitment? Why do you think the commitment level is low?"

- "Who are not currently your customers, but could be?"

- "To what degree is mutual respect a part of staff interactions with one another? Why is this so?"

- "What would you need to do to enhance significantly how your organization functions?"

- "What forces for change are acting on your organization now? What forces for stability are acting on your organization now? What challenges does this situation present you for the future?"

- "What pleases you about this organization? What upsets you about it?"

- "What do you find confusing about how our organization functions?"

  Variation: Substitute other words and phrases for the word "confusing": "surprising", "gratifying", "interesting", "supportive", "unsupportive".

- "Think about your work group over the past year. Has anything changed significantly about how people work together?"

6

- "What do you find satisfying about working here? What frustrates you about working here?"

- "What do you like most about being a member of this group? What do you like least about being a member of this group?"

- "How do you know when you have been successful? unsuccessful?"

- "What do our customers say about our service?"

- "How does the public view your organization?"

- "There are two kinds of issues: the ones we talk about and the ones we don't talk about. What issues do we talk about? What issues do we not talk about?"

- "If we were to close our doors tomorrow, who would miss us? Why would they miss us? Who would not miss us that we wish would miss us? Why would they not miss us?"

- "What issues are important to people with lesser status and power in our organization? When will these issues be included in the discussion?"

- "As a senior manager, what keeps you awake at night when you think about the future of our organization?"

More Questions on Identifying the Issues:

6

Understanding the Issues

- "Describe the problem facing us as a challenge in a single sentence. For example, 'The challenge is to …' or 'The real issue is …' or 'Our priority is to …'"

- For whom is this issue a problem? How is it a problem?

  Tip: Chapter 5, Questions for Thinking Critically has a number of questions that are also effective for analyzing issues.

- "What makes this problem complex for our organization?"

  Variations: "What makes this problem interesting? What makes this problem a challenge for our company? What makes this problem urgent for us?"

- "What is going on now that pulls down our customer satisfaction ratings?"

  Probes: "Who are our customers? What do we know about them? What features of our products are most important to our customers? How do we know that?"

- "Who else (other than your team members) is connected to this issue (problem)?"

  Probe: "How can they influence the outcome?"

- "How comprehensive are we being in trying to understand this issue?"

  Probes: "Are we taking a holistic perspective and looking at the big picture or do we have just one small part of the big picture? How will we know that we have a comprehensive view?"

- "This looks like a pretty negative situation. Where is there a potential silver lining?"

- "What feedback have we received from our customers recently – for example, letters of satisfaction and support, complaints, comments about service and so on – that pertain to this problem?"

- "What is going on now that should not be happening? What should be going on now that is not happening?"

- "How does this problem (issue, challenge) affect you?"

  Probe: "How does it affect you personally? in terms of your job? your family life?"

- "What are the benefits to you for getting this issue resolved this year?"

- "How are these issues related to our organizational values?"

- "If you were selecting a product like ours for your home, who would be our competition? What would encourage you to select a competitive product?"

- "What will happen if nothing is done to address this problem?"

- "What is the history of this issue in our organization?"

  Probe: "When did this issue emerge? What helped it grow? How did we respond? Whom did we consult? What have we learned so far?"

- "Where is our greatest vulnerability in relation to this issue?"

  Tip: When a problem occurs, ask why it occurred. Ask the question, "Why?" as many times as it takes until you get at the systemic cause of the problem. (The Japanese teachers of quality would have you ask "Why" five times.) [51]

- "How inclusive are we in our approach to understanding this issue? Whose perspective is being excluded?"

- "For the best result we need everyone's wisdom on the table. Whose wisdom are we missing?"

- "What employee cultures are involved in this issue? Are you including their approaches in trying to understand this issue?"

- "What incentives are there to solve this problem? Are there any benefits for not addressing this problem?"

- "What makes you nervous about addressing this issue? What makes you feel good about addressing this issue?"

6

- "Who is responsible in our formal and informal organizational structures for providing leadership in addressing this problem?"

- "What is your personal bias about this issue?"

   Probes: "What is it based on? What other personal biases are present? What are they based on?"

- "Do we have all the background information we need to address this problem?"

- "What is not being said about this issue that needs to be said?"

- "What pressures are there for us to address this issue?"

> *That which you ignore Will rise up and strike you.*[52]

- "How will the politics in our organization have an impact on this issue?"

- "What opportunities are there for us in this area?"

- "What turning points (key events) have we experienced over the past year in relation to this issue?"

- "How does this challenge fit within your strategic plan (mission, vision, values, priorities, goals)?"

- "What data (both quantitative and qualitative) do you have that will help you understand these challenges?"

- "What are the top three factors that contribute to making this a problem for us?"

- "How does this issue disrupt things in our community/organization/ group?"

- "What is it about this issue that you may be ignoring at your peril?"

- "How is social justice, or other broad and comprehensive issues, tied into these concerns?"

More Questions on Understanding the Issues:

6

Generating Options for Action

- "In what ways are we stuck? What do we need to do to get unstuck?"

- "What could you do to raise your level of customer satisfaction so that your customers are delighted with your products and services?"

- "What do you hear people complaining about most in relation to this issue? What could we do immediately to address some of these complaints? What could we do over the longer term to address these complaints?"

- "What is the one thing we can do now that will have the biggest possible impact on our success over the coming year?"

- "What's unchangeable about this problem?"[53]

  Probe: Review the response in terms of hidden assumptions or biases.

- "What are some polarity traps (opposites) we could get into with respect to this issue, that is 'either we do this or we do that'?"

  Probe: "Thinking in polarities reduces both our creativity and our options. What other options do we have that take us away from these polarities?"

- "Who has faced this problem before? What did they do? What were the results?"

  Probe: "Has anything been written about best practices or benchmarks in relation to addressing this problem in other organizations?"

- "What are the consequences of not addressing this issue?"

- "What is there about our organization (for example, systems and policies) that enable this problem to continue?"

- "What is a relatively small problem that you can fix now that will have a major positive impact on your customers?"

- "What would it take to deal with this issue?"

- "How is solving this problem relevant to our customers? Our employees? Our shareholders? Our board members?"

> *The external situation is never the real problem. It's how we relate to that situation that's important.*[54]

- "Was this activity intended to be an experiment or a real-time application?"

- "What symptoms indicate that you have a problem? What are the sources of these symptoms?"

- "What are the most obvious solutions to this problem? What are the least obvious solutions to this problem?"

- "What opportunities does this issue present us with?"

- "What other approaches to this problem have you seen (heard about, wanted to explore)?"

- "What action(s) can we take as next steps that will resolve the conflict?"

  > *Tip: Actions represent what each party will do as a result of the discussion, What by Whom by When.*[55]

- "Are all options possible or are specific approaches being discouraged?"

- "In many situations involving complex, long-standing issues there are a few people who are keen about trying out new approaches. Who might these people be in your situation? What are their perspectives?"

More Questions on Generating Options for Action:

6

Testing Options for Action

- "Which of these approaches do you feel most comfortable endorsing? Why?"

- "If you take this step, where are you vulnerable?"

- "What are the benefits and drawbacks of each of these options in relation to your organization?"

- "Is a pilot project needed to test this approach?"

- "How comfortable are you with this approach?"

- "Can you live with this solution?"

- "What stands out about this option that makes it the best solution?"

- "How much disruption will this issue cause? How will this disruption likely happen?"

- "Who is likely to benefit from this solution? Who is likely to pay the cost for this solution?"

- "Who might want to protest this option at a political level?"

- "Where is this solution most vulnerable, that is, if something could go wrong, what would it be?"

- "What do you like most about this solution? What do you like least about this solution?"

- "What values does your organization have that are in support of this solution? What values does your organization have that are not in support of this solution?"

- "Do you get the sense that we are on the same wavelength here, or are we missing each other?"

- "I'm curious about your reasons for taking this approach. Can you remember how this solution was suggested?"

- "Which option do you prefer? What are your reasons for supporting this option?"

- "Which option offers the best chance for success?"

- "If we make this change now, what are some potential immediate, mid-range and long-term impacts for our customers?"

  Variation: Substitute other words for "customers": "shareholders", "employees", "contributors", "donors".

- "How will we know that we have successfully addressed this issue?"

  Probe: "What will be different from today?"

More Questions on Testing Options for Action:

_____

_____

_____

_____

_____

_____

6

Making a Decision

- "What is the decision that you need to make?"

    Probe: "Complete the following sentence: 'We need to decide ...' "

- "Whom should you consult with before making this decision?"

- "How (group consensus, group vote, senior management authority) should you make this decision?"

- "What could prevent you from making a decision about this issue? What factors are supporting you to make a decision now?"

- "Who will make the decision?"

- "Is anyone missing from this discussion who might have a different perspective? What would this person tell us if she were here?"

- "What are the potential downsides of this decision? How can you accommodate these factors?"

- "What criteria (e.g., our values, norms for working together, impact on employees, impact on the public, impact on our stakeholders) can guide us in making our decision?"

- SCAMPER is a problem-solving technique for use at decision points. The following questions are considered:

    S   What can be Substituted?

    C   What can I Combine?

    A   What can I Adapt?

    M   How can I Modify or Magnify?

    P   What can be Put to other uses?

    E   What can be Eliminated?

    R   What is a Reverse of the item or what Rearrangement can be made?[56]

6

- "Who will be affected most (or least) by this decision? How will they be affected?"

- "When does this decision need to be made? Is timing important to the outcome? If yes, how? If no, why not?"

  Following is a pattern of questions facilitators can use with groups to help them make decisions.

  1. *"What are you going to decide?"*
  2. *"Who will make the decision?"*
  3. *"What criteria will you use to make your decision?"*
  4. *"Who is affected by your decision?"*
  5. *"When must you make your decision?"*
  6. *"What tool will you use to make your decision?"*
  7. *"What is your decision at this time?"*[57]

- "Who is happy with this solution? Who is not happy?"

- "What are the ethical implications of this decision?"

- "What is the best way (e.g., consensus, voting, multi-rating) to make this decision?"

  Building a lasting consensus is a critical phase in this meeting. Once you have completed the last step in this process, ask group members the following questions:

  - *"Can you live with this action?"*
  - *"Will you support this action within the group?"*
  - *"Will you support this action outside of the group?"*

  If anyone is unable to answer "yes" to any of the above questions, then ask that person to answer the following question:

  - *"What has to change in order for you to support this action?"*

  Continue with the decision-making discussion until a proposal is made that meets the conditions for desired changes.[58]

6

More Questions on Making a Decision:

Taking Action

- "What is the first thing we need to do to get this solution off on the right foot?"

- "What are the top two or three changes that will really challenge productivity while you are moving your headquarters? What do you have going for you that will help you adapt to these changes? What weaknesses does your organization have now that will cause problems in relation to these changes?"

- "Where are the traps along the path ahead of us?"

- "Whom should we involve to support us in being successful?"

- "What can we do to facilitate positive politics inside our organization in support of this solution?"

- "If people are going to resist this solution, what form will that resistance likely take?"

    Probe: "What is the likely cause of this resistance and how can we address it?"

- "Who should champion each of the major aspects of this implementation process?"

- "How can we get our stakeholders involved in the implementation process?"

- "How will this solution affect you personally at work? Focus on specific consequences."

    Variation: "How will this solution affect you at home? Focus on specific consequences."

Joseph A. Atkinson, founder of the Toronto Star daily newspaper, wrote on May 1, 1940 that there are four things an executive should know:

1. *What ought to be done?*
2. *How should it be done?*
3. *Who should do it?*
4. *Has it been done?*

6

- What are all the possible ways that this decision could be sabotaged internally? Externally?

    Probe: Generate a plan for addressing these roadblocks.

More Questions on Taking Action:

_____

_____

_____

_____

_____

_____

6

Recommended Reading

Block, Peter. *Stewardship. Choosing Service Over Self-Interest.* San Francisco, CA: Berrett-Koehler, 1993.

Francis, Dave and Don Young. *Improving Work Groups: A Practical Manual for Team Building.* (Revised) Toronto, ON: Pfeiffer and Company, 1992.

Kaner, Sam, et al. *Facilitator's Guide to Participatory Decision-Making.* Gabriola Island, BC: New Society Publishers, 1996.

Mosvick, Roger and Robert Nelson. *We've Got to Start Meeting Like This!* Glenview, IL: Scott, Foresman and Company, 1987.

Reddy, W. Brendan. *Intervention Skills: Process Consultation for Small Groups and Teams.* Toronto, ON: Pfeiffer and Company, 1994.

The Kidney Foundation of Canada. *Advocacy Handbook.* Montreal, QC: KFOC, 1999, www.kidney.ca.

Weaver, Richard G., and John D. Farrell. *Managers as Facilitators.* San Francisco, CA: Berrett–Koehler, 1997.

6

Chapter 7

Questions For Closing a Session

Although they are often neglected, closings are as important as openings.

At the end of a single session or a longer process involving multiple meetings, the challenge for facilitators is to bring closure to the process. Participants need to be able to reflect on what they have accomplished and on what they want to do next in relation to their objectives.

Closing questions help participants re-enter their day-to-day work patterns in the context of the meeting or workshop they have just completed. Thus, closing questions are often bridges between the end of one process and the beginning of another, for example, the end of strategic planning and the beginning of operational planning.

Closing questions are provided for three areas:

1. reflecting on the process – perspectives on the experience, midway through a process, productivity and celebrating success

2. considering next steps

3. debriefing.

As mentioned in the preface to this book, the questions in this chapter are designed for verbal interactions during sessions. Questions for written approaches, or for prior to or after sessions, are included in other ST Press publications.

Guidelines for Closing Questions

Closing questions are transitional – they provide the key to addressing unfinished business and moving on. They also provide special opportunities for learning as participants close their "files" on a process, put them away and decide what they are going to do next.

Use the blank space at the right-hand side of the page to check off the guidelines that you would like to emphasize more.

a.   Create closing questions that support participants in bringing an end to a process. These questions assist participants in summarizing what they have achieved and what they have not achieved with respect to their stated objectives: "What did we do best during this process? What could we have done better?"   _____

b.   When appropriate, ask questions that reflect the fact that some participants may need to grieve the end of a process; others may be glad to see it ending. If you are bringing closure to a lengthy and involved process where people will no longer be seeing each other, some participants may want to discuss their feelings about leaving each other or communicating less frequently, or they may want to set up a network.   _____

c.   Ensure that responses to closing questions feed into the client–consultant debriefing meeting for a project: "If you were the facilitator for this session, what is one thing you would do differently next time?"   _____

d.   Use questions that encourage recognition of the contributions of everyone involved in the project or meeting: "What did you learn from each other – your colleagues – during this project?"   _____

e.   Develop questions that enable participants to feel included as legitimate members of the group: "What is one contribution or perspective that you brought to the table?"   _____

7

f. Where appropriate, provide an opportunity for participants to respond to these questions in a confidential manner, for example, through an anonymous, written questionnaire. _____

g. Use questions that provide an opportunity for participants to disclose their concerns, anxieties and areas of disagreement in a non-threatening, low-anxiety manner: "You can help us learn by describing how this process went for you. What did you like most about this session? What did you like least about this session?" _____

h. Use a question pattern that moves participants through the *"What? – So What? – Now What?"* framework (see *Chapter 4, Questions for Enabling Action*), and provides a positive and motivating link into next steps or future sessions. _____

i. Ensure that the time allotted for the closing is appropriate given the relationship between what people will say and how it ties into the session objectives and overall purpose.

    In some situations, the answers to closing questions need to be extremely short, perhaps 5 to 10 seconds per person. For example, "Let's go around the table and say what single word or phrase describes your experience here today. Give us the first one that comes to mind right now; don't think about it. It's okay if your word is the same as someone else's." _____

7

Reflecting on the Process

More than one wise person has commented on the fact that an unexamined life is not worth living. And so it goes with processes and facilitation. The following questions encourage reflection by participants during the middle and closing parts of a process. Questions are provided for four areas: perspectives on the experience, midway through a process, productivity and celebrating success.

Focus: Perspectives on the experience

- "What are the first words that come to mind to describe how you felt when this session started? What are the first words that come to mind to describe how you feel now?"

  Suggestion: If you use the first question during the opening, refer to those responses at the end.

- "How clear was the purpose of this session during the first few hours?"

- "What did you like most about this meeting? What did you like least about this meeting?"

  Tip: This question also works well for long-term project closings. For example, "What did you like most (or least) about being involved in this project over the past six months?"

- "What benefits did you experience as a result of being involved with this project?"

- "Overall, how did this process go for you?"

  Probe: "What were the strong and weak parts of it from your perspective?"

- "What's one good thing that happened for you today? What's one not-so-good thing that happened for you today?"

- "What did this session feel like to you?"

- "What stands out most in your mind about this session?"

- "What do you know now that you didn't know when this process started?"

- "On a scale of 1 to 5, where 1 is poor and 5 is excellent, how would you describe today?"

  Probes: "What made you pick that number? Is this the number you usually pick to describe your days or do the numbers vary? Do you want to change this number for tomorrow? What could you (or we) do to change this number for tomorrow?"

- "What influences outside your work environment had a positive effect on your experience as a team member for this project? What influences outside your work environment had a negative effect on your experience as a team member for this project?"

- "If a couple of your best friends were going to come into this account planning session next year, what advice would you give them about how to have a successful and enjoyable planning session?"

- "How well did we listen to each other throughout this process?"

- "Are you comfortable with how disagreements and conflicts were handled by group members? Please explain."

- "How creative were we in our approaches to issues?"

  Variations: Substitute other words for "creative": "timely", "focused", "candid", "pragmatic".

- "Would you describe the level of conflict on your team during this project as low, medium or high? Please explain your response."

- "How comfortable were you with the level of participation by group members?"

  Probe: "Did people participate equally? Did some people avoid participating?"

- "When (how often) did personalities get in the way of constructive problem solving?"

- "From your perspective, how does a really excellent process differ from one that is second-rate?"

  Probe: "How did this process compare?"

- "What themes kept emerging in discussions during the last part of the process?"

  Probe: "Why do you think these themes became dominant?"

- "Do you feel any different about yourself as a team member after working on this project for six months?"

- "What could have made this experience more meaningful for you?"

- "After participating on this team for an entire season, what do you think are the coach's key values or deeply held beliefs about working with high performance athletes?"

  Variation: Substitute "manager" or "leader" for "coach" and adjust the end of the question to suit your situation.

- "How was disagreement or conflict handled in your small group?"

  Probes: "What was your level of comfort with conflict among group members? Was it dealt with constructively? Were there situations where it became destructive?"

- "How did other participants contribute to your experience during this course?"

  Probe: "What did they contribute that both helped you and hindered you in having a successful and enjoyable course?"

- "Looking back on this process, what's the good news? What's the bad news?"

- "In hindsight, what two or three core values guided how your group functioned?"

7

More Questions Focused on Perspectives:

Focus: Midway through a Process

- "What is one thing that stood out for you during today's session?"

- "If you could change one thing about today's session, what would it be?"

- "What are you going to focus on during tomorrow's session?"

- "What were your recurring thoughts during today's small group session?"

    Probe: "Did your thoughts help or hinder your participation and focus?"

- "What is one thing you can learn from someone else in your group during the time remaining in this process?"

    Probe: "How will you learn this?"

- "On a scale of 1 to 4, where 1 is poor and 4 is excellent, how would you describe today?"

    Probes: "Do you want to change this number for tomorrow? What could you (or we) do to change this number for tomorrow?"

- "What possible ethical issues, if any, do you see emerging?"

- "What was the most relevant part of this experience for you?"

- "What are you going to focus on in relation to _____ as a result of participating in this session?"

    Variations: Use the "What? - So What? – Now What?" framework (see Chapter 4) to set up these questions.

More Questions for Midway Through a Process:

7

154

Focus: Productivity

- "During the introductions you were asked about your hopes and concerns for this meeting. How did the meeting turn out for you in terms of what you had hoped for?"

- "How did your group make key decisions? Did this work well?"

- "How did the small group session work for you, that is, were you in a stimulating and productive group or not?"

- "What were your goals at the beginning of the day? To what extent did you achieve them?"

- "On a scale of 1 to 4, where 1 is not successful and 4 is successful, how successful was this session in terms of productivity from your perspective? Please explain."

    Variations: Substitute other words or phrases for "how successful was this session": "how well did this session meet our objectives", "how healthy were your interactions as group members".

- "Which of your norms for working together helped your group the most in terms of productivity? Why?"

- "What is one thing you have learned from working with the people on this team? What do you think you have learned as a team within your larger organization?"

- "What did you contribute to the session's outcomes (to the group's productivity)?"

- "What is one thing you learned about information technology planning through your involvement in this project?"

    Variations: Substitute other words or phrases for "technology planning": "social support networks", "leadership development", "strategic planning", "project management".

7

- "Have you achieved the objectives (outcomes) stated at the beginning of this process?"

    Probe: "If yes, how do you know? If no, what else needs to be done to achieve these objectives (outcomes)?"

More Questions Focused on Productivity:

_____

_____

_____

_____

_____

7

Focus: Celebrating success

- "How can we formally declare that this project is now completed?"

  Variation: "How can we celebrate the conclusion of this project?"

- "Whom do we want to acknowledge for their effort and accomplishments in making this event successful?"

- "What is one 'takeaway' or significant benefit you got out of today's session?"

- "Are there other areas of our organization or related organizations that would appreciate learning from our experience?"

  Variations: "What have we learned that will be applicable to other companies? How is our experience relevant to those with whom we collaborate? Are we in partnerships or alliances that would appreciate hearing about our experience?"

- "How can we celebrate what we have accomplished? How can we celebrate how we worked together?"

- "Is there a journal or magazine that would be interested in a short article describing our experience and what we have learned from this process?"

- "What is one thing of value that you are walking away with as a result of participating in this process?"

- "What parts of your involvement in this program did you find the most fun?"

  Probe: "What happened that made them fun?"

  Variations: Substitute other words for "fun": "productive", "enjoyable", "educational", "stimulating", "troubling".

7

More Questions Focused on Celebrating Success:

Considering Next Steps

People who attend a lot of meetings, planning workshops and training sessions can get quite cynical about the value of these processes if there is no follow-up action based on what was accomplished. The following questions help to bridge between the process and the action.

- "What 'unfinished business' do you think this group still needs to address?"

- "What do we need to discuss to be able to move on?"

- "How interested are you in continuing your involvement with the next steps in this process?"

- "Would you like to be involved in the implementation part of this process? If yes, please explain how you might contribute. If no, please explain why not."

- "What is one thing you will do as a result of this session when you are back in your office?"

- "We made the final decision in this session by _____. How comfortable are you with how we made this decision?"

- "What other organizations are you aware of that might benefit from your experience in and conclusions to this process?"

  Probe: "Would they like to meet with us to share experiences, lessons learned and areas for mutual growth and development?"

- "How can we share what we have learned from this project with others inside and outside our organization who could benefit from our experience?"

- "So – what do we need to do next here?"

7

- "You have just spent two days discussing how our company acts on its corporate social responsibility in this community. If you were in charge of this organization, what is the first thing you would do to act on the results of this session?"

  Probe: "How can we support this happening when we are not in charge?"

- "What are you most concerned about now that this process is over?"

- "If you were in charge, what is one thing you would do to build on the work that has been done?"

- What legacy would your team like to leave behind for your organization?

- "Now that this project is completed, we, as project team members, will be taking the results of our work back to our various departments in the company. How do we want to talk about what happened during this start-up phase? What can we do as a group to support a common leadership message about resource planning in our company?"

  Tip: Project teams often play a large role in an organization in relation to implementation. Common messages can help support the next steps in implementation.

- "What is the single most important factor that will determine whether our organization is successful in acting on the recommendations we have created through this process?"

More Questions for Considering Next Steps:

Debriefing

Remember to use your rules for good feedback to ensure that the debriefing doesn't become superficial or negative.

Debriefing sessions, sometimes called post mortems, need to be planned and facilitated carefully. The feedback and experience gained from dissecting a process are invaluable to our development and maturation as facilitators. Following are sample questions for debriefing meetings with clients.

- After distributing completed evaluation sheets to the organizational team, ask, "What do our evaluations say about how this project went? If you were planning a project similar to this one, what would you do differently?"

    Probe: "What would you do the same?"

- "How does our final product (result) compare with our initial ideas and objectives?"

    Probe: "Have we kept on track? Are these differences improvements or problems?"

- "If a colleague asked you what you learned from being involved in this session, what would you say?"

- "From your perspective, what was this group best at? Where was this group weakest?"

- "What helped us? What hindered us?"

- "You have been approached by an auditor who is investigating the usefulness of this process in relation to the amount of money invested in making it happen. What would you say to the auditor?"

- "In what ways did the room setup contribute to or detract from a successful workshop?"

7

- "Hindsight takes reflection to become 20/20. If you were facilitating this process next year, what would you change? What would you keep the same?"

- "Now that we have completed our discussions on _____ , how confident are you with the decisions we have made?"

- "If you were the senior manager looking back on this project, what is one thing you would do differently that would make a significant positive difference to the outcome?"

- "Did we have the right people involved to achieve our stated objectives? If yes, please describe the roles (skills, characteristics) required that were fulfilled by team members. If no, please suggest additional roles (skills, characteristics) required."

- "Did you have the support (e.g., human and financial resources, technology, political) required for this process to be successful? Please explain."

- "What was your favourite part of this process? What part of this process did you like the least?"

- "Was there anything in our approach that you found frustrating?"

- "What have we learned that we can take forward into the next session on this project?"

  Probe: "What would we do differently? What would we keep the same?"

More Questions for Debriefings:

_____

_____

_____

_____

7

Recommended Reading

Brady, John. *The Craft of Interviewing*. New York, NY: Vintage Books, Random House, 1976.

Everton, Neil. *The VJ Handbook*. A survival guide for any new journalist in a multi-skilled newsroom. Toronto, ON: Canadian Broadcasting Corporation Training and Development, P.O. Box 500, Station A, Toronto, ON. email: tortrain@toronto.cbc.ca

Fairhurst, Gail and Robert Sarr. *The Art of Framing*. San Francisco, CA: Jossey-Bass, 1996.

Hoff, Benjamin. *The Tao of Pooh*. New York, NY: Penguin, 1982.

Payne, Stanley L. *The Art of Asking Questions*. Princeton, NJ: Princeton University Press, 1951.

7

Chapter 8

Questions for Specific Cases

This chapter describes responses made to facilitators about questions for specific cases. These cases were raised during training workshops or coaching sessions.

Opening a Workshop on a Specific Topic

Situation: *I often facilitate sessions that focus on a specific topic such as leadership, mentoring or benchmarking. This means that during the opening part of the session I have to think about how to introduce the topic and also begin to drive towards objectives and outcomes at the same time. How do you do this?*

I have found the following questions helpful in sessions that focus on a given topic. The examples are listed under specific topics, but can be adapted for use with other topics.

Learning from leadership

- "Think about your experience to date as a senior leader in your organization. What is a key learning you have had about organizational leadership in your working life? State your learning as a commandment."

    Tip: When leaders respond to a question like this one there is enough risk involved to both support group development and enhance ownership for the outcomes of the session.

Organizational leadership

- "What is a challenge that your organization (or another organization you know) is currently facing in relation to leadership?"

    Tip: The option in brackets encourages disclosure without a breach of confidence.

National corporate leadership

- "What is at stake in our country in relation to corporate leadership at the national level?"

Mentoring

- "You have been asked to act as a mentor to a new employee who is a young, recent graduate of an MBA program. What are the top two pieces of advice you would give this young man to help him be successful in your company?"

Ethics and issues

- "What ethical questions do you bring to the table on this issue?"

    Tip: Explaining words such as "ethical" ensures that the responses will tie into your objectives.

Performance management

- "If you could change one thing about how this company rewards employees – other than increasing financial rewards – what would it be?"

Team development

- "What is your most important contribution to this team to date? What do you get from this team?"

Program review

- "What is one good thing about this program so far? What is one not-so-good thing about this program so far?"

8

Workplace feedback

- "What is one thing about ethics (or service, marketing, etc.) in this organization that you are proud of? What is one thing about ethics (service, marketing, etc.) in this organization that needs to be improved?"

Perspectives and challenges

- "When you look at this situation from the perspective of a ___ , what are the main challenges?"

Problem definition

- "Describe the two biggest problems in this project as catchy newspaper headlines."

Priority setting

- "What are your top two criteria for funding projects in this area?"

Consensus building

- "Where do you think the greatest area of agreement is with respect to resolving this issue? Where do you think the greatest area of disagreement is with respect to resolving this issue?"

Financial success

- "What does it take to be successful financially in this company?"

- "What was your first paid job? What would you like your last paid job to be?"

Values clarification

- "In what ways are you a conformist? A non-conformist?"

- "If you saw someone stealing something from a store, would you intervene? Why or why not?"

- "Are you materialistic? If so, how? If not, why not?"

8

Personal development

- "What is one bad habit that you have broken during your lifetime?"

- "What is a risk that you feel comfortable taking that others you know might not feel comfortable taking?"

- "What qualities do you want in a friend?"

- "If you won the lottery, what would you do with the money?"

- "If you could accomplish one significant thing over the next year, what would that be?"

See *Chapter 3, Questions for Opening a Session* for more suggestions.

Opening a Series of Workshops

Situation: *When we facilitate several workshops or meetings that happen over a period of time, that are in a limited series or that involve scheduled reunions of groups, the opening questions are often based on hindsight about what has happened in previous sessions. Can you suggest some questions that work well in these situations?*

One approach is to focus on what was learned previously as a way to encourage participants to think about what they want to learn at the new session. For example:

- "What did you get out of your last meeting with group members?"

- "What do you want to get out of this meeting?"

Another approach is to focus on the personal responsibility of individuals in taking ownership for a productive and enjoyable experience as a group member:

- "At our last meeting we set the following norms for working together to ensure that the session would be productive and enjoyable. Given your experience at our last meeting, which of these norms do you think is most important to ensuring a positive experience for you this time around?"

- "What did we do well at our last meeting in terms of group norms? What do we need to focus on this time around?"

At a recent graduate school alumni reunion in the United States, participants from 25 years of classes were asked to sit in groups according to their graduating class, develop a group response to three questions and record their responses creatively in the flip chart space provided on the wall. Each class had its own section of a 25-year timeline spread out along two walls. There were two flip chart pages for each class.

The questions were:

1. What was going on in the business world when your class was in session? (key events or incidents)

2. Describe briefly a defining moment or a highlight for your class.

8

3. Provide a word, phrase, symbol, picture or drawing that reflects the essence of your class.

This opening activity took about three hours for all classes to complete, including process time in plenary. It provided thumbnail insights into each class over a 25-year period, helped classes build ownership for their unique experience as they presented their overview to other classes and enabled them to see snapshots of the school's entire history in an afternoon.

The activity seemed to have just the right amount of risk to support rapid group development during this first reunion for alumni. Most of the professionals at this graduate school are comfortable with fairly high levels of risk in terms of group process and would have been disappointed by an opening activity that didn't challenge them in some significant way.

Several classes were explicit about the intense frustration they experienced during a period of upheaval and disorganization in the university's administration. Other classes celebrated what was for most of their students a life-changing learning experience. One class talked about the lack of bonding in a year when expectations about intellectual intimacy were not realized. A recent graduating class used this activity to explore why their experience was not of the quality they had expected.

As a participant-observer at this event, it seemed to me that these questions elicited powerful, insightful responses that enabled plenary group development and brought closure to the past while opening up avenues for future learning. The questions also fed directly into the objectives for the reunion, which were focused on learning from the past and building for the future. As each class presented its perspective on the past, it was enlightening to watch other classes run through a gamut of responses such as joy, frustration, concern, surprise, confusion, disappointment or mutual support.

8

Bringing a Project to a Close

Situation: *I am an external management consultant who has just completed the implementation of a new information technology (IT) re-engineering process in a national firm with nine locations in our country. This process has happened over three months.*

The process began with all nine teams together at a national, two-day meeting. Then we worked with each team on-site to support them in providing local leadership.

We are bringing the nine teams together again in two weeks to discuss how the project has unfolded and to bring closure to this training process at that meeting. Four internal human resources (HR) people will also be present at this meeting. The IT project will be formally handed over to these nine teams for implementation. Each team has five to seven members, depending on the size of their location.

What questions might be helpful at this closing session?

The first step is to consult with internal HR personnel to find out what they want to get out of this closing session. There are several possible purposes for this session:

- to bring formal closure to the project
- to thank team members for their efforts
- to provide a venue where the president can make a formal presentation to reward successful team work
- to develop a report on lessons learned so that the CEO can share this information with other CEOs at the quarterly international executives' meeting
- to end the project on a positive note
- to explore unfinished business among team members and between teams
- to bring everyone together in a joint learning session
- to think about next steps in maintaining and enhancing the new IT approach on an on-going basis.

8

If the purpose of the meeting is to acknowledge and celebrate what the teams have accomplished, you may want them to sit in their work teams to address questions at the beginning of the meeting and then move them out of those teams during further discussions. In this way, they have an opportunity to be acknowledged as a working group and to celebrate their accomplishments and then to move on to re-identify with the larger group towards the end of the session.

The questions in teams could ask them to reflect on their experiences in working together, for example, what the key challenges were and what they can celebrate now that their work is completed. The questions in the larger group could provide feedback to Human Resources for future projects of this scope: "Given hindsight, if you were in charge, what is one thing you would do to enhance the ability of team members to work together efficiently and happily?"

Following are further sample questions for this closing session, depending on your purpose. Some of these questions may also be appropriate for a written questionnaire sent to participants before the actual session.

- "Here are the objectives for this closing session. Do these seem appropriate to you? Please comment, making additions or deletions if you wish."

- "What went well on this project?"

- "What do we still have to work on?"

- "What did you like most about being a member of your location's team?"

- "If you had to do this all over again next week, what is one thing you would change?"

- You have been hired away from this company to another firm where you will be the Director of Human Resources. Your first major task is to develop and implement a process similar to this one. "What have you learned from this process that will help you in your new job?" State each learning in a single sentence as a commandment, beginning with a verb.

8

Closing a National, Issues-based Workshop

Situation: *I am facilitating a national workshop on transportation issues for an arms-length Crown corporation. There are 45 participants from all sectors of the economy: private, public, union, non-government groups and charities. What suggestions do you have for closing questions?*

In situations similar to this one, we have set some closing questions and then met with a representative volunteer from each sector during the final workshop break to ensure that the questions are appropriate. A representative planning committee might also be a good place to test the questions.

Taking a consultative approach to developing these questions helps to ensure that you will avoid bias or an accusation that the questions were set to make the workshop outcomes look good.

- One approach is to ask people to sit in their sector teams and come to agreement in 10 minutes on responses to the following questions:

    - "What is one thing that stood out for you at this meeting in relation to how people worked together?"

    - "What message will you be taking back to your sector's organization?"

    Then ask a volunteer from each sector team to present the results to the total group. You can close with the committee chair thanking the participants, presenters and others and reviewing the agreed next steps.

- The closure to a workshop is often the ending of one phase and the starting up of another. Workshops usually generate work for specific people, and there is a need to communicate with those who weren't there. An important question to ask is "How can we communicate with others who aren't here to ensure that they hear about the workshop and its impact on their part of the country?" One approach is a phone-tree: Each person contacts one or two other people to tell them about the results of the workshop. As part of your debriefing activity, you can develop the key points that would be part of what people tell one another.

8

- At a national network meeting where the purpose was to extend the network from a fairly closed partnership of four large agencies to a broader partnership involving a variety of 17 agencies (also in the workshop), we asked people who represented all the agencies in the room to deliver the closing remarks by talking about one thing they learned at the event and how they thought their organization would want to participate in the network in the future.

The closing piece in a process provides a final opportunity to reflect and further the purpose of the event. This closing furthered the goals of the workshop by emphasizing the importance of an inclusive approach. In addition, it avoided having the original four larger partners, who gave the opening remarks, also giving the closing remarks. The approach worked well; several people commented on how powerful they found the closing comments of the 17 participating agencies.

Conducting Exit Interviews in Small Groups

Situation: *I am the coach of a national women's field hockey team. This year we are dropping six athletes from our roster: One athlete has been the team captain for three years; two athletes have been on the team for four years; two athletes are subs and have had very little match playing time. I am going to conduct final interviews with the athletes in small groups and am having difficulty thinking of suitable questions. Can you help me out? How should I set this up?*

Athletes and coaches learn a lot through their participation in sport. Both you and they can benefit from sharing those learnings and passing them on to future coaches and athletes. Interviews that wrap up an athlete's career are important for several reasons:[59]

- Athletes will be better able to integrate the value of their athletic experience into their lives after sport if they are encouraged to reflect on its potential impact and meaning.

- Athletes who reflect on and value their experience in sport may be potential coaches; no sport can afford to overlook an opportunity to encourage the future involvement of former athletes.

- Final interviews provide an opportunity for you to address "unfinished business," that is, challenges that you and the athletes may have experienced and not talked through completely.

How you describe these group interviews and how you plan to use the feedback will influence the quality of participation. Be sure to explain that these are confidential small group discussions (see the section *Clarifying confidentiality* in *Chapter 2, Core Facilitation Values*), that you will be reporting back to the entire team (including those interviewed) with an anonymous summary of what was said and that you will be integrating as many suggestions as possible with next season's team. Give a couple of examples of changes you will be making.

8

Here are some suggested questions:

- "What were you looking for when you first got involved in field hockey?

    Probes: "Have you found what you were looking for? Has what you were looking for changed or evolved while you were playing?"

- "What are some positive things that have happened to you as a result of your participation in field hockey?"

- "What are some negative things that have happened to you as a result of your participation in field hockey?"

- "If you could change one key thing you did during your participation in field hockey, what would it be?"

- "If you could experience one thing again that you experienced while you were participating in field hockey, what would that be?"

    Probe: "Do you want to share these feelings with others who were involved with you at the time?"

- "Do you have any regrets about your participation in field hockey?

    Probes: "What things did you do that you might have done differently? Do you have any bad feelings about others on the team? Do you need to have any closing discussions with people on the team about things that happened?"

- "What were some highlights for you as an athlete in field hockey?"

- "What did you learn about yourself as a result of participating in field hockey?"

- "What did you learn about coaching as a result of participating in field hockey?"

- "Overall, on a scale of 1 to 6, where 1 is poor and 6 is excellent, how would you describe your experience as a field hockey player? Please explain your choice of number."

8

- "Think of all the coaches you have had. Pick one who was particularly effective. In your view, what was it about that coach that made him effective?"

- "Think of all the athletes you have known during your experience in sport. Pick one that you especially admire. In your view, what is it about that athlete that makes her admirable?"

- "Was it your choice to get involved in field hockey or was someone else a key motivator?"

- "What did you learn as a result of your experiences in field hockey that you can apply in other situations?"

- "Sport creates many pressures for athletes. Describe one positive and one negative pressure that you experienced."

- "If you had a child who wanted to get involved in field hockey, what would you consider before signing her up?"

- "If you were developing a training program for coaches, what courses come to mind as being most important?"

8

Enabling a Structured Approach to Reflection and Action

Situation: *The groups I work with are not good at dialogue. After reviewing a report they argue, debate and posture, but they don't really explore new learning or action. Can you suggest some questions that would help with this problem?*

Create explicit and focused questions that guide discussion through the *"What? – So What? – Now What?"* framework. Create opportunities for as much air time as possible, building agreement in stages from pairs or trios to the larger group.

> *We are not good at balancing advocacy and inquiry. Most of us are educated to be good advocates. While there is nothing wrong with persuasion, positional advocacy often takes the form of confrontation, in which ideas clash rather than inform.*[60]

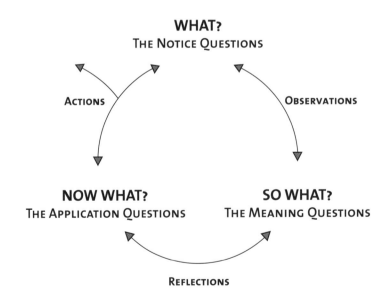

What?

- In trios: "What main conclusions did you see woven throughout this report? Share individual impressions and come to agreement on the top two conclusions."

So What?

- "Does your experience as a senior manager support these conclusions? Note a couple of examples to illustrate your point of view."

- "On a scale of 1 to 5, where 1 is completely in agreement and 5 is not in agreement at all, indicate the degree to which your organization is in line with these conclusions. Please explain your choice of number."

Now What?

- "What is one change you could make in your organization that would build on the conclusions in this report and have a significant, positive effect on employees?"

8

Encouraging Candour and Confidentiality

Situation: *I often facilitate in situations where I want to encourage candour and confidentiality in support of mutual disclosure. What kinds of questions can I ask to enable an environment where people will share this kind of information?*

Many facilitated sessions depend on participants disclosing information about their own situations without breaching confidentiality. This can present participants with a dilemma: They want to participate in meaningful discussion but at the same time they don't want to betray confidential information about their organization to competitors(see the section *Clarify confidentiality* in Chapter 2). They may also not want to portray their organization in a negative light.

Although setting a norm for candour can be a good start, facilitators may find that it doesn't work unless the questions used during the session follow up that norm by stimulating appropriate disclosures from participants.

> *"You can tell your paper," the great man said,*
> *"I refused an interview.*
> *I have nothing to say on the question, sir;*
> *Nothing to say to you."*
> *And then he talked till the sun went down*
> *And the chickens went to roost.*[61]

A climate that supports appropriate disclosure is one in which ground rules for confidentiality are in place, information sharing is a norm, the facilitator models appropriate information sharing (e.g., not disclosing names of other clients, upholding mutual respect, not taking unreasonable risks), questions are constructed to "protect" the participant while she is disclosing information and mistakes are seen as opportunities for significant learning.

Following are sample questions that support participants to disclose appropriately:

- "What's one thing you know for sure about this issue?"

- "What is one thing you learned as a result of your experience as a senior manager in large organizations?"

8

- "Most managers today are experiencing a lot of stress in relation to____ . Do you also find this challenge in your organization? What symptoms do you notice?"

- "What is one perspective you are hearing about these days in relation to these issues?"

- "If you could predict the top two (human resource) issues for organizations like yours over the next five years, what would they be?"

- "From your perspective, what is at stake here for our employees?"

8

Exploring Legislation That Impacts on Organizational Policies

Situation: *We are discussing the impact of new tobacco legislation at an upcoming senior managers' meeting in our national, heart health, non-government organization (NGO). This legislation will arrive on our desks the day before we need to discuss it. What are some questions we could use to explore the legislation and guide our discussion and decision making?*

Ensure that everyone has had the time to read the legislation and to reflect on its implications. You may want to provide 5 or 10 minutes at the beginning of the meeting for people to review the legislation and jot down their responses to the first question before initiating discussion.

Use the *"What? – So What? – Now What?"* framework to guide the development of questions.

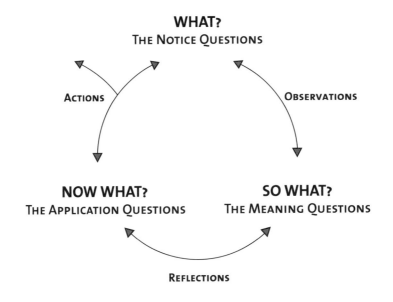

WHAT?
THE NOTICE QUESTIONS

ACTIONS

OBSERVATIONS

NOW WHAT?
THE APPLICATION QUESTIONS

SO WHAT?
THE MEANING QUESTIONS

REFLECTIONS

8

What?

- Post the organization's mission at the front of the meeting room: "What are the first words that come to mind to describe this legislation with respect to our organization's mission?"

- "What stood out for you about this potential legislation when you think of our new capital project?"

So What?

- "Here is a list of our organization's priority projects over the next two years. How will the key aspects of this bill affect these projects?"

- "Which of these impacts (if any) will be beneficial for us? How? Which of these impacts will cause us problems? How?"

- "How will this bill have an impact on society at large? Do any potentially positive social benefits (e.g., increased employment) outweigh any concerns we may have?"

Now What?

- "What are our options for action in relation to this legislation?"

- "Which of these options will we take? What is the first step to ensure a positive outcome for our NGO?"

8

Loosening Up A Tight Group

Situation: *I am facilitating a week-end strategic planning retreat for a very successful, conservative, primarily male law firm that prides itself on its establishment image. What questions can you suggest for opening the first evening of this workshop for 30 partners?*

We have found that planning retreats for professional firms often include the usual strategic planning objectives as well as a combination of firm "team development" issues, partner conflict management problems and questions related to the future direction of the firm. The sooner we can set and implement norms for how issues will be identified and addressed, the better the planning process will proceed. We usually gather considerable information about the firm prior to the retreat and then use that information as a basis for questions during the opening session.

Following are some sample opening questions that we have used successfully for a variety of professional firms in areas such as law, medicine, accounting, education and dentistry. These questions all depend on workshop participants having received prior to the workshop a confidential and anonymous report on interviews or questionnaires completed by the firm partners. Be sure to ask questions that include just the right amount of risk and disclosure for encouraging participants to begin to build ownership for the overall process.

Questions related to the report:

*   "What stood out for you on your first reading of this report?"

*   "How did you feel when you finished your first reading of this report?"

*   "What common threads do you see weaving through this report?"

*   "What do you think someone from another firm would conclude about your firm after reading this report?"

    Probe: Are these conclusions accurate?

8

- "Would you provide this report to someone who was a new hire? Why or why not?"

- "This report provides a snapshot in time of your firm based on interview questions that the planning committee developed with us. For how long has this been a snapshot of your firm?"

- "What do you like most about the image of your firm? What do you like least about the image of your firm?"

- "What is there in this report that makes you feel optimistic about your future? What is there in this report that makes you question the future of the firm?"

- "The objectives for this session were developed prior to this report. After reading this report, do the objectives for this session still seem reasonable or do we need to fine tune them?"

Further questions:

- "From your perspective, what is a key element in your vision of this firm three years down the road?"

- "What needs to happen at this retreat to make it successful from your perspective?"

- "What is one piece of information related to the future of the firm that you think it is important for everyone to keep in mind during this planning session?"

- "What is one norm for working together as partners that you think needs to be in place to ensure that this workshop is successful?"

- "Think of a planning retreat that you participated in that was a success from your perspective. What made it successful? Think of a planning retreat that you participated in that was not successful from your perspective. What made it unsuccessful?"

  Suggestion: Turn the responses to this question into a list of norms for working together.

8

Putting Sensitive Issues on the Table

Situation: *What questions can I ask to get perspectives about a sensitive issue (such as gender) on the table during a mixed (male and female) group discussion?*

Split the group into two subgroups: one of men and one of women. Ask each subgroup to complete a given sentence by making a list on a flip chart.[62] The women's subgroup completes the sentence: "In our society, being a woman means that … " The men's subgroup completes the sentence, "In our society, being a man means that …" (Customize the sentence to suit your situation.)

Then each subgroup presents its list, and the facilitator asks participants to comment on impressions, surprises, omissions, additions and so on while discussing similarities and differences between the two lists.

The purpose of this activity is to explore differences, not to create arguments about what is right or wrong or which way is best. When there are different points of view, acknowledge them and continue with the discussion rather than trying to resolve them.

8

186

Reflecting on and Applying Research

Situation: *I work at a national think tank that produces research papers for review by senior leaders in organizations at international conferences. In the past we simply did the research, produced the paper and then convened workshops and conferences for discussion purposes. Our customers want more now: They want to be able to apply what is in these research papers to their work situations. What are some questions we could ask that would stimulate discussion in relation to applying the information in these research papers?*

It sounds as if you (the think tank) are moving from presenting information to encouraging your customers (senior leaders in organizations) to explore relevant content and apply it to their work situations. Depending on the size of the group involved, the following questions based on the *"What? – So What? – Now What?"* framework may be directed in various ways (e.g., to an entire group, to a small group, for consideration as part of a task, in preparation for a presentation, etc.).

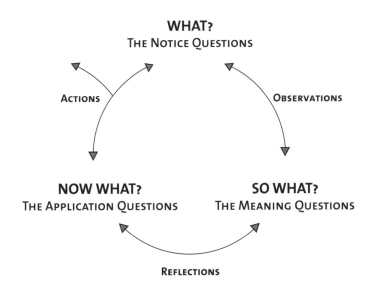

8

What?

- "What was your first reaction after reading this report?"

    Probe: "Did anyone else have this reaction? What is this reaction based on?"

- "What is one question that surfaced for you after reading this paper?"

- "If you could add a section to this paper, what would it be called?"

So What?

- "When you think about the kinds of issues your organization is facing now, do these conclusions seem relevant?"

- "What does your experience and intuition say about the relevance of this research to your organization?"

- "Does this report take into consideration the social and political context in which your organization is functioning today?"

- "What sort of real, back-home issues in your life are related to what is discussed in this paper?"

- "If you could have a private lunch with the author of this paper and ask her anything you wanted, what are two questions you would ask?"

- "When you think about organizations like yours, would these recommendations do more good than harm? How do you know?"

- "If you acted on the key conclusions in this paper in your company over the next six months, what risks would surface in relation to your bottom line?"

- "From your perspective, what are the top two or three assumptions underlying this report?"

    Probe: "Do you agree with these assumptions? Why or why not?"

- "Think about leaders you respect in your area of work. How would they view this report?"

   Probe: "What parts of this report would you like to discuss with them? Why?"

- "Is your experience similar to that of the authors or different from theirs? Please explain."

- "Would publication of this report make a difference in your area of work? Why or why not?"

- "In what ways do the conclusions of this report reflect your experience? In what ways do they not reflect your experience?"

Now What?

- "What impact do you think the conclusions in this report will have on your field over the short term? Over the long term?"

- "What is one insight you gained from reading this paper and discussing it with your peers? How might this insight serve as a catalyst for change in your organization?"

- "What 'truths' about your organization are reflected in the conclusions and recommendations in this report? How could you act on these conclusions and recommendations to improve how your organization functions?"

8

Reviewing a Pilot Workshop

Situation: I am looking for some questions to ask participants at the end of a one-day pilot workshop on benchmarking. This workshop will be refined based on feedback and then offered at multiple sites to middle managers, all of whom have to participate in a workshop within a four-month period.

When introducing questions, remind participants that this is a pilot workshop that will be reviewed, refined, and then offered at other sites. Ask them to contribute their expertise to the review process by responding to your questions. Choose three or four questions that will directly assist in your review process.

- "As you know, we are going to be providing this workshop to all middle managers over the next four months. We want to build ownership and commitment to using benchmarking on a regular basis. What advice do you have for us as organizers now that you have completed this session?"

- "Will you change anything in terms of how you act back home based on your participation in this workshop?"

    Probe: Ask for specific examples.

- "What is one question about benchmarking you had that was answered during this workshop? What is one unanswered question you have at the end of this workshop?"

- "Given your experience, what do you think are the key points that facilitators should be emphasizing in this workshop?"

- "What do you think is the main factor in your company that will determine whether benchmarking is an overall success?"

    Probe: "What can we do through these workshops to ensure that this factor gets addressed?"

8

- "How will you report back to your supervisor on this workshop?"

- "How you will portray this workshop to other managers? Why?"

- "Are you interested in co-facilitating a workshop based on a revised agenda?"

- "Can you recommend other managers at your level who might be interested in co-facilitating these workshops?"

8

Supporting Action After a Meeting of a Network or Coalition

Situation: *What questions can I use to bring an action oriented ending to our province-wide green environment network meetings?*

We sometimes find it helpful to teach the *"What – So What – Now What"* framework to participants as a way to raise awareness about where an agenda is to move during a network meeting. This usually takes about 10 minutes. As a rule, participants like learning the framework and can see uses for it in many situations, both personal and professional.

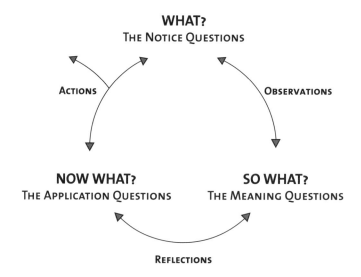

Once participants understand the framework, you can use questions such as the following to close your network meetings and support next steps.

What?

- "What stood out during this meeting for you in terms of our current emphasis on …?"

So What?

- "How does this observation fit with our current goals for this area?"

Now What?

- "What are the implications regarding what we have learned here today for us as individuals, community members and network members?"
- "What is one thing we can all do as network members over the next month to support our network's current emphasis on …?"

8

Thinking Critically About Policy Changes

Situation: *We are moving our government's support for physical fitness programs and classes to a broader approach called Active Living. What can we do to help our policy group think critically about this transition and the ways in which our new policy on Active Living will be different from how we have worked in the past under a narrower physical fitness approach?*

We prepared the following bank of questions as a starting point for the policy group to think critically about Active Living and thus deepen their understanding of the concept. Group members selected questions from the following list to frame their discussion.

The basics

- "How can we describe Active Living? Why the term? Who for? How is it unique? What is the role of physical activity in Active Living?"

- "What do we (government) want to achieve with Active Living?"

- "How do we know that living actively enhances well-being?"

- "Is there a typical prescription for Active Living? If so, can you describe it?"

- "Is Active Living a measurable concept? If so, how do you measure it? If not, what are the implications of driving a concept that can't be measured?"

- "Are there minimum standards for Active Living?"

- "Should people be more active? How do we address exercise intensity through Active Living?"

- "What does the concept of Active Living include? Does it go beyond being active physically and include being active as a community leader? Are there any guidelines for defining Active Living?"

8

- "What are some examples of Active Living?"

- "Is Active Living a new fad?"

- "How does the notion of personal empowerment fit with the concept of Active Living?"

Links to other areas

- "Does Active Living include work-related physical activity as well as leisure time physical activity?"

- "Is Active Living supported by existing social norms and values?"

- "How can physical activity be an important feature of activities that are essentially mental, social or spiritual?"

- "What is the relationship between Active Living and the environment? Health? Recreation and leisure? Sport? The workplace?"

Active Living and fitness

- "Is Active Living just fitness with the name changed?"

- "Does cardiovascular fitness remain an important issue?"

- "When fitness was the goal, individuals knew when they were fit. How do people know when they are living actively?"

- "Does Active Living include performance goals?"

- "Has the definition of physical activity changed?"

The department's role

- "How does Active Living fit with our department's current Blueprints for Action?"

- "What are the implications of Active Living for existing departmental policies, programs, activities and organizational structures?"

8

- "What is the process for incorporating Active Living into our department's current activities?"

- "How do we manage this change process?"

- "What could Active Living look like over the next two years?"

- "Will Active Living be a new program in our department?"

- "What is the difference between Active Living and our department's current health promotion initiatives?"

Implementation

- "Should we continue to encourage Canadians to move along a continuum from minimum-level physical activity to more intense, regular physical activity?"

- "If freedom of choice and individual 'fit' are inherent in the concept, does it mean that each individual should have access to a full range of opportunities?"

Leadership

- "What is the best role for our department with respect to Active Living?"

- "Will Active Living result in an enlarged mandate for our department?"

- "How will group fitness leaders be involved in Active Living initiatives?"

- "If Active Living focuses on the individual, who is responsible at the group level for Active Living?"

Programs

- "If the concept of Active Living suggests that individuals can incorporate any type of physical activity (such as walking) into their daily lives, is there still a need for structured programs?"

- "Does implementing Active Living require additional resources (time, money, knowledge, equipment, space, social organization)?"

8

Promotion and communication

- "What is the process for communicating Active Living to other government departments? Health related organizations? The public in general?"

- "What is the difference between promoting participation in physical activity in accordance with a fitness concept and in accordance with the Active Living concept?"

8

Workplace Stress: Encouraging Candour and Action

Situation: *I am leading a stress management workshop for union stewards in my company. This is a very "stressful" topic in our macho environment. Participants have just completed a questionnaire on personal stress levels. How can I get them to feel comfortable about disclosing their scores and working on strategies for enhancing how they manage stress in this environment?*

First, normalize the range of scores on the instrument and the fact that everyone experiences and deals with stress differently. Second, emphasize that there is no way to avoid stress – it is a normal, predictable part of every person's life. Third, disclose your own scores on the instrument for a time in your life that was very stressful.

Another approach that we have found powerful is to plot scores anonymously on a wall chart when people are not in the room. This visual approach can be a powerful stimulant for discussion.

With either approach, you can then work through *the "What? – So What? – Now What?"* framework with questions like the following.

What?

- "What is your score? Does this score make sense to you given your current personal and work situation?"

- "What is one thing that stands out for you when you look at your results?"

So What?

- "What does this score say about the amount of distress you are experiencing in your life now? Is it manageable? Unmanageable?"

- "What is one thing that you see other people doing in relation to time off and stress management that you would like to do in your life? What is preventing you from doing this in your life?"

    Probe: "What supports do you have in your life in relation to this goal?"

Now What?

- "Given your situation at home, what is one thing you could do now or over the next 24 hours that would make a positive difference in relation to anxiety and tension in your life?"

- "Whom can you count on to support you in making this change? What does this person need to do to be supportive of your decision? How will you talk to this person about the changes you want to make?"

- "What is the first thing you will do personally to get started on this change?"

8

Endnotes

1   C. Roland Christensen et al., *Education for Judgement: The Artistry of Discussion Leadership* (Boston, MA: Harvard University Press, 1991), 156. Reprinted by permission of Harvard Business School Press. Copyright 1991.

2   George M. Gazda et al., *Human Relations Development. A Manual for Educators,* 3rd ed. (Toronto, ON: Allyn and Bacon, 1984), 142-45. Adapted by permission. Copyright 1984 by Allyn and Bacon
Dorothy Strachan, *Nobody's Perfect Training Manual* (Ottawa, ON: Federal Government Ministry of Supply and Services, 1988).

3   Stanley L. Payne, *The Art of Asking Questions* (Princeton, NJ: Princeton University Press, 1951), 116. Reprinted by permission of Princeton University Press.

4   Stanley L. Payne, *Rogue's Gallery of Problem Words*, Chapter 10, quoted in Seymour Sudman and Norman M. Bradburn, *Asking Questions: A Practical Guide to Questionnaire Design* (San Francisco, CA: Jossey-Bass, 1982), 49.

5   Christensen et al., 158. Adapted.

6   Paul Tomlinson and Dorothy Strachan, *Power and Ethics in Coaching* (Ottawa, ON: Coaching Association of Canada, 1996), 49. Adapted.

7   Ken Metzler, *Creative Interviewing*, The Writer's Guide to Gathering Information by Asking Questions (Englewood Cliffs, New Jersey: Prentice-Hall, 1977), 41-42. Adapted.

8   These tips come from personal experience and two main sources:
(a) Phillip Hunsaker and Anthony Alessandra, *The Art of Managing People* (New York, NY: Prentice-Hall, 1980), 95-101. Adapted.
(b) Strachan, 175-76.

9   Christensen et al., 162.

10   Chris Argyris. *Intervention Theory and Method: A Behavioral Science View* (Reading, MA: Addison-Wesley, 1970), as quoted in Roger M. Schwarz, *The Skilled Facilitator* (San Francisco, CA: Jossey-Bass, 1994), xvi.

11   John Heron, *Group Facilitation: Theories and Models for Practice.*(London, UK: Kogan Page, 1993), 16.

12   Sam Kaner et al., *Facilitator's Guide to Participatory Decision-Making* (Gabriola Island, BC: New Society Publishers, 1996), 24.

13   See the IAF web site at www.iaf-world.org.

14   Kaner et al., x.

Endnotes

15   Roger M. Schwarz. *The Skilled Facilitator.* (San Franscisco, CA: Jossey-Bass, 1994), 5.

16   Schwarz, 15. Adapted.

17   David A. Garvin, "A Delicate Balance: Ethical Dilemmas and the Discussion Process", in *Education for Judgment* (Boston: Harvard University Press, 1991), 288. Adapted.

18   Dorothy Strachan and Paul Tomlinson, *Gender Equity in Coaching* (Ottawa, ON: Coaching Association of Canada, 1996), 7.

19   Theodore Roethke. "Journey to the Interior" in *The Collected Poems of Theodore Roethke.* (Toronto, ON: Doubleday, 1975), 189.

20   Christensen, xv. Adapted.

21   Robert W. Terry, *Authentic Leadership: Courage in Action* (New York, NY: Jossey-Bass, 1983), 114-126. Adapted. Reprinted by permission of Jossey-Bass, Inc., a subsidiary of John Wiley and Sons, Inc. Copyright Jossey-Bass, 1983.

22   Terry, 67.

23   B.W. Tuckman, "Development Sequence in Small Groups", in *Psychological Bulletin, 1965,* 284-399.

24   John Brady, *The Craft of Interviewing* (New York, NY: Vintage Books), 85-86.

25   Several writers have explored Experiential Learning in terms of behavioural change, e.g., Newell et al (1960), Miller et al (1960), Pounds (1969), Kolb (1971), Marks and Davis (1975), Pfeiffer and Jones (1975 and 1980), Argyris (1976, 1985), Gaw (1979), as well as Wheeler and Marshall (1986) in relation to training styles. Pfeiffer and Jones refer to "so what" and "now what" questions in "Introduction to the Structured Experiences Section" in *The 1980 Annual Handbook for Group Facilitators* (La Jolla, CA: University Associates, 1980), 3-8.

26   Neil Postman and Charles Weingartner, *Teaching as a Subversive Activity* (New York, NY: Delacorte, 1969), 23.

27   Beverly Gaw. "Processing Questions: an Aid to Completing the Learning Cycle," in *The 1979 Annual Handbook for Group Facilitators* (La Jolla, CA: University Associates, 1979), 149. See also the introduction to "Structured Experiences" in *The 1980 Annual Handbook for Group Facilitators* (La Jolla, CA: University Associates, 1980), 3-8. Some of the questions in this section come from these articles; most are from our experience in the field. For another perspective on experiential learning related to research paradigms, see Shulamit Reinharz, "Implementing New Paradigm Research: a Model for Training and Practice," in *Human Inquiry*, edited by Peter Reason and John Rowan (Toronto, ON: John Wiley and Sons, 1981), 417–32. For yet another perspective, see R. Brian Stanfield, ed., *The Art of Focused Conversation* (Toronto, ON: New Society Publishers, 2000), 18-20.

28   R. Brian Stanfield, ed., *The Art of Focused Conversation* (Toronto, ON: New Society Publishers, 2000), 10.

29 Clark E. Moustakas, *Finding Yourself, Finding Others* (Englewood Cliffs, NJ: Prentice-Hall, 1974), 57.

30 Stephen D. Brookfield, *Developing Critical Thinkers* (San Francisco: Jossey Bass, 1987), 232. Reprinted by permission of Jossey-Bass, Inc., a subsidiary of John Wiley and Sons, Inc. Copyright Jossey-Bass, 1987.

31 Ray Bradbury, *Fahrenheit 451* ... The Temperature At Which Books Burn (New York, NY: Ballantine Books, 1950), 164.

32 Peter Senge, *The Fifth Discipline. The Art and Practice of The Learning Organization* (New York: Doubleday/Currency, 1990), 159.

33 Brookfield, 22.

34 Peter R. Scholtes, *The Leader's Handbook* (Toronto, ON: McGraw-Hill, 1998), xiii.

35 Wislawa Szymborska, *View with a Grain of Sand.* "An Opinion on the Question of Pornography". (Orlando, FL: Harcourt Brace and Company, 1995), 159.

36 Paul Tomlinson et al. *A Resource Manual for AIDS Educators.* (Ottawa, ON: Canadian Public Health Association, 1991), 18.

37 Brookfield, 165.

38 Tomlinson et al, 12. Adapted.

39 Brookfield, 67.

40 David Dotlich and Peter Cairo, *Action Coaching* (San Francisco, CA: Jossey-Bass, 1999), 249.

41 Donald A. Schon, *Educating the Reflective Practitioner* (San Francisco, CA: Jossey-Bass, 1987), 7. Reprinted by permission of Jossey-Bass, Inc., a subsidiary of John Wiley and Sons, Inc. Copyright Jossey-Bass, 1987.
    E. Hughes, "The Study of Occupations," in R.K. Merton, L. Broom and L. S. Cottrell, Jr., eds., *Sociology Today* (New York, NY: Basic Books, 1959).

42 Brookfield, 120-121. Adapted.

43 Dietrich Bonheoffer, "Suum Cuique," quoted in John Dalla Costa, *The Ethical Imperative: Why Moral Leadership Is Good Business* (Harper Collins, 1998), 175.

44 R. Brian Stanfield, *The Courage to Lead* (Gabriola Island BC: New Society Publishers, 2000), 173.

45 Patricia Clar, "Business Ethics: A Balancing Act," *The United Church Observer,* 57 (7), 18-23 (1994).

46 John Dalla Costa, *The Ethical Imperative: Why Moral Leadership Is Good Business* (Harper Collins, 1998), 203.

47 Dalla Costa, 258. Adapted.

Endnotes

[48] The Kidney Foundation of Canada, *Advocacy Handbook* (Montreal, QC: KFOC, 1999), 3-1. www.kidney.ca

[49] For more information on comprehensive, inclusive, whole system approaches, see Peter Senge, *The Fifth Discipline. The Art and Practice of The Learning Organization* (New York, NY: Doubleday/Currency, 1990), R. Brian Stanfield, *The Courage to Lead* (Gabriola Island, BC: New Society Publishers, 2000) and Peter Scholtes, *The Leader's Handbook.* (Toronto, ON: McGraw-Hill, 1998).

[50] Brookfield, 115-16.

[51] Scholtes, 266.

[52] Holzer, Jenny as quoted in Stanfield, *The Courage to Lead,* 136.

[53] Kaner et al., 198.

[54] Stanfield, *The Courage to Lead,* 55.

[55] Richard G. Weaver and John D. Farrell, *Managers as Facilitators (*San Francisco, CA: Berrett–Koehler, 1997), 113. Reprinted with permission of the publisher. All rights reserved. 1-800-929-2929.

[56] Michalko (1991) building on the work of Alex Osborn and Robert Eberle. Quoted in Reddy, W. Brendan. *Intervention Skills: Process Consultation for Small Groups and Teams.* (San Diego, CA: Pfeiffer and Company, 1994), 155.

[57] Weaver and Farrell, 103-4.

[58] Weaver and Farrell, 124. Adapted.

[59] Paul Tomlinson and Dorothy Strachan, *Power and Ethics in Coaching,* 64-65. Adapted.

[60] Stanfield, *The Art of Focused Conversation,* 8.

[61] O. Henry, as quoted in John Brady, *The Craft Of Interviewing* (New York, NY: Vintage Books, 1977), frontispiece.

[62] Tomlinson et al.,109-110. Adapted.